MELITO OF SARDIS

On Pascha

T0339012

ST VLADIMIR'S SEMINARY PRESS
Popular Patristics Series
Number 55

The Popular Patristics Series published by St Vladimir's Seminary Press provides readable and accurate translations of a wide range of early Christian literature to a wide audience—students of Christian history to lay Christians reading for spiritual benefit. Recognized scholars in their fields provide short but comprehensive and clear introductions to the material. The texts include classics of Christian literature, thematic volumes, collections of homilies, letters on spiritual counsel, and poetical works from a variety of geographical contexts and historical backgrounds. The mission of the series is to mine the riches of the early Church and to make these treasures available to all.

Series Editor
JOHN BEHR

Associate Editor
AUGUSTINE CASIDAY

MELITO OF SARDIS

On Pascha

With the Fragments of Melito and Other
Material Related to the Quartodecimans

Translated, Introduced, and Annotated by
ALISTAIR C. STEWART

ST VLADIMIR'S SEMINARY PRESS
YONKERS, NEW YORK
2016

Library of Congress Cataloging-in-Publication Data

Names: Melito, Saint, Bishop of Sardis, active 2nd century, author. |
Stewart, Alistair C. (Alistair Charles), 1960– author of introduction,
annotator, translator.
Title: On Pascha : with the fragments of Melito and other material related to
the Quartodecimans / translated, introduced, and annotated by Alistair C.
Stewart
Other titles: Peri Pascha. Greek
Description: Second edition. | Yonkers, New York : St. Vladimir's Seminary
Press, 2017. | Series: Popular Patristics series ; Number 55 | In English
and Classical Greek; English text of Melito is translated from Classical
Greek. | Includes bibliographical references and index.
Identifiers: LCCN 2016046622 (print) | LCCN 2016047379 (ebook) | ISBN
9780881415544 | ISBN 9780881415551
Subjects: LCSH: Jesus Christ--Passion--Sermons--Early works to 1800. | Bible.
Gospels--Relation to the Old Testament. | Quartodecimans. | Sermons,
Greek--Early works to 1800.
Classification: LCC BT430 .M413 2017 (print) | LCC BT430 (ebook) | DDC
252/.63—dc23
LC record available at https://lccn.loc.gov/2016046622

COPYRIGHT © 2016 BY
ST VLADIMIR'S SEMINARY PRESS
575 Scarsdale Road, Yonkers, NY 10707
1-800-204-2665
www.svspress.com

ISBN 978–088141–554–4 (paper)
ISBN 978–088141–555–1 (electronic)
ISSN 1555–5755

PRINTED IN THE UNITED STATES OF AMERICA

*for Alice
with love*

Contents

PREFACE TO THE FIRST EDITION   9
PREFACE TO THE SECOND EDITION   11

INTRODUCTION   13
   Melito   13
   On Pascha   20
   Sardis   23
   Melito the sophist   24
   The Quartodeciman liturgy and Melito's *On Pascha*   28
   The Quartodeciman Pascha and the Jewish Pesah   33
   Melito's anti-Judaism   37
   The theology of Melito   39
      a) Melito's doctrine of God in Christ   39
      b) Eschatology   41
      c) Typology   42
   Conclusion: Melito's liturgical theology   45
   Further Reading   45
   Editorial Note on the Greek Text   49

On Pascha   50

THE FRAGMENTS AND OTHER MATERIAL   85
   a) Fragment 1   85
   b) Fragment 2   87
   c) Fragment 3   88
   d) Fragment 4   89
   e) Fragment 5   89
   f) Fragment 7   90
   g) Fragment 8b   90

h) Fragments 9–11   92

i) Fragment 14   94

j) Fragment 15   96

k) Fragment 16b   98

l) Fragment 17   98

TESTIMONIA TO MELITO FROM LATER AUTHORS

a) From Eusebius   101

b) From Jerome   102

SELECTIONS FROM OTHER AUTHORS CONCERNING
QUARTODECIMAN PRACTICE

a) Apollinarius   105

b) Hippolytus   107

c) Eusebius (includes long quotations
    from Polycrates and Irenaeus)   108

d) From the *Life of Polycarp*   115

e) From the Syrian *Didascalia*   116

f) From Theodoret   118

g) From *Epistula Apostolorum*   120

INDEX OF MODERN AUTHORS   123

INDEX OF ANCIENT AUTHORS   125

Preface to the First Edition

This work is not a scientific translation of *On Pascha*, but a fairly free rendition intended for students, seminarians, working clergy, and faithful Christians. I would hope that this audience would get an idea of the contents and style of *On Pascha*, and some indication of its significance, particularly with regard to our understanding of the earliest paschal liturgy. In translating I have had a view to the rhetorical quality of the text, and in particular to the fact that the piece was designed to be spoken aloud, and scientific accuracy was therefore prized less highly than euphony.

The text employed is that of Hall, who also provides an excellent translation; my debt to Hall's work will be manifest on every page and those requiring an apparatus and accuracy at every point should turn to Hall, rather than to the present work. The reader will also find frequent reference to my work *The Lamb's High Feast*, published two years ago; I have taken the opportunity here to correct some of the less guarded statements found in that work, particularly with regard to Hippolytus, and to expand on a few points, particularly with regard to Melito's *eunouchia* (as a result of a conversation with colleagues in a tea-shop!).

The class on "The Jewish Roots of Christian Liturgy," taught at the General Seminary in New York in 2000, was subjected to some of this material, and even managed to make some contributions to the effort. The manuscript was proof-read by Gloria Bowden of the Diocese of Atlanta, and the editor of this series, Dr John Behr, showed diligence and patience in equal measure in preparing it for the press.

I have been studying Melito since 1987, assisted by his prayers and those of all the saints, and continue to find new depths in his work. I hope that through this work my audience will be able to share something of this pleasure. In time I hope that the dedicatee will be part of the audience.

New York
On the feast of Saint Alban, Protomartyr of Britain, 2000

Preface to the Second Edition

Responding to the request of St Vladimir's Seminary Press for a second edition of this work incorporating the Greek text of *Peri Pascha* has been both painful and pleasurable. It has been pleasurable to immerse myself once more in Melito's work, though painful to discover how dated some aspects of my discussion of Melito in my 1998 work now appear (although published in 1998 the earlier parts are the product of the late 1980s). However, I continue to hold that the overall argument is sound, and have taken the opportunity to issue a brief defense of the major conclusions of the work.

Beyond adding the Greek text and partially revising the introduction, I have taken the opportunity to improve the appendix by expanding the number of fragments included and to update the testimonia to Quartodeciman practice in the light of more recent research. The translation of *On Pascha*, however, is virtually unaltered.

Particular thanks are due in this second edition to Stuart Hall for his consent to my use of his Greek text, and to Darrell Hannah for sharing his translations of the *Epistula Apostolorum*. There is no new dedicatee; the infant daughter of 2000 is now a reader of this work, and of much else besides, most of which is beyond her father's comprehension.

"Peace to the writer, and to the reader, and to those who love the Lord in simplicity of heart" (colophon, Bodmer codex of *On Pascha*).

Chalvey, Slough
On the Feast of St Ignatius of Antioch, 2015

Introduction

Melito

Late in the second century, Victor, then leading bishop in Rome, sought to gain some unity in the manner in which the mystery of the Lord's death and resurrection was celebrated in Rome. Rome was not a united church at the time but a loose federation of churches, and immigrant groups tended to keep their ancestral customs. Asian Christians in particular kept a festival on the fourteenth day of the Jewish month of Nisan, at the same time as the Jewish Passover, at which they commemorated the death and resurrection of the Lord. In time they became known as Quartodecimans, since they kept the fourteenth day, but this usage, deriving from the Latin quarta decima, which means "fourteenth," is later.

It is hard to determine all the details of Victor's involvement in the Quartodeciman controversy, but somehow the Asian bishops were drawn into the dispute. Eusebius writes of Victor as a monarch bishop claiming a rather wider jurisdiction than he actually held, summoning synods in the various Asian cities.[1] It is more likely that Asian communities in Rome, whose customs were being questioned by Victor, the leading elder among the churches, looked to their ancestral homeland for support and assistance. One of the traditional duties of the leading bishop (among others) in Rome was correspondence with other churches, which is the capacity in which Clement writes to the Corinthians in the letter known as *I Clement*, and so as "foreign secretary" Victor, once the Asian bishops had been

---

[1]Eusebius, *Ecclesiastical History* 5.23; this document may be found below on p. 108.

drawn in, would have become even further involved, and his further involvement would increase Eusebius' impression that Victor was "Pope," or single bishop of Rome. Whatever the manner in which he became involved, a letter from Polycrates, bishop of Ephesus, to Victor is recorded by Eusebius, in which are mentioned notable figures who had kept Pascha on the fourteenth of Nisan. Among them is mentioned "Melito the eunuch who governed entirely in the Holy Spirit, who lies at Sardis. . . ."[2]

We may deduce a number of significant points about Melito from the letter of Polycrates. First, we may deduce that Melito was a Quartodeciman, that he kept Pascha on the fourteenth of Nisan in accordance with the custom that had been handed down from Judaism.[3] Second, we may note that, compared to the other authorities whom Polycrates cites, such as Philip and John the apostles, Melito had but recently died at the time in which Polycrates wrote. If this is the case we may date his death to *c.* 190. Hall dates Melito's *Apology* fairly precisely between 169 and 177, and, on the basis of a notice in Eusebius with which we shall deal below, he dates *On Pascha* uncontroversially, though by no means certainly, between 160 and 170.[4] We may accept his dating for the *Apology*, but shall suggest that the notice in Eusebius is of little help in dating *On Pascha*. Nonetheless we may gather from the dating of the *Apology* and from Melito's position in Polycrates' catalogue that Melito flourished in the third quarter of the second century.

Third, we may deduce from Polycrates' statements here that Melito was Jewish by birth. Polycrates lists seven great lights of

[2]Quoted by Eusebius, *Ecclesiastical History* 5.24; this letter may be found below on p. 110.

[3]Although some voices have been raised doubting that Melito was indeed a Quartodeciman, or suggesting that the work here attributed to Melito of Sardis is the work of a different author altogether, this need not detain the reader of this introduction. For details and bibliography see A. Stewart-Sykes, *The Lamb's High Feast: Melito, Peri Pascha and the Quartodeciman Paschal Liturgy at Sardis* (Leiden: Brill, 1998), 2–3, 6–7.

[4]S. G. Hall, *Melito of Sardis: On Pascha and Fragments* (Oxford: Clarendon, 1979), xii with reference to Eusebius, *Ecclesiastical History* 4.26.1.

Asia who had been Quartodecimans and then adds himself as a "supernumerary eighth." The particular great lights enumerated by Polycrates have been chosen for some reason, and Bauckham suggests that they are named because Polycrates is claiming that he is himself related to all of these in some way. Polycrates indeed states that those mentioned are all his relatives (*suggeneis*).[5] But this of itself does not explain why Polycrates should wish to point out his network of relationships. Normal classical usage employs the term *suggenēs* ("relative") and its cognates to mean relationships within an extended family or within a nation, and to refer to relationships between families claiming a connection or states claiming a common origin, and actually excludes close blood-relationship. This is the probable sense in which Polycrates employs the term. The only possible set of relationships to which Polycrates may be referring is Jewish; Paul uses the same term to refer to fellow-Jews when he speaks in Romans of his relatives according to the flesh.[6] Polycrates' argument is then not only that seven great Asian lights, including the apostle John, were Quartodeciman, but by implication that this is an ancient practice derived from Judaism. Melito was Jewish by birth, an attribute which he shares with a number of significant leaders of the Asian Christians.

Fourth, we may also deduce from Polycrates' writing that Melito was bishop in Sardis. Hall notes that, whereas Polycrates names some as bishops, Melito is not given this distinction, and suggests that the identification of Melito as bishop is the work of Eusebius.[7] Whereas we may agree with Hall that Eusebius' description of Melito as bishop is certainly beside the point, we may note that those described as bishops in Polycrates' list are also martyrs, and it may be this double qualification that causes him to employ the term at this point. Moreover, Polycrates does state, elsewhere in his letter,

[5]Richard Bauckham, "Papias and Polycrates on the Origin of the Fourth Gospel," *Journal of Theological Studies* 44 (1993): 24–69, at 29–30.

[6]Rom 9.3.

[7]Hall, *Melito of Sardis:On Pascha*, xii.

that Melito was bishop. After his mention of the seven great lights of
Asia (the last of whom is Melito) who kept the fourteenth, Polycrates
goes on to say: "seven of my relatives were bishops." These are the
seven who kept the fourteenth day and who were fellow Jews with
Polycrates. Melito is among them as bishop. Moreover, Polycrates
refers to Melito "governing all things in the Holy Spirit." Lawlor and
Oulton translate this phrase as "lived in the Holy Spirit" and take
it as a reference to Melito's piety.[8] Although "living" is a possible
translation of the Greek verb *politeuomai*, we would not expect an
object (*panta*); the word is, however, used with an object by classical
authors to refer to systems of government, or to the act of governing, and on this basis we may suggest that Polycrates is speaking of
Melito's governance of the church in the Holy Spirit. Mindful of what
was said above, however, regarding Victor's episcopate, we must
clarify that Melito was probably not a bishop in the modern sense,
but was head of a single Christian household or school.

Finally, we must deal with Polycrates' puzzling description of
Melito as "the eunuch." Early in her treatment of the parallel proso-
pographies of Favorinus and Polemo, the former of whom was a
eunuch, Maud Gleason writes:

> Congenital eunuchs are a rare phenomenon and eunuchs of
> any sort were probably not a daily sight in the provincial cities
> of the western empire at this time, or even in the east, where
> self-castrated priests were traditionally associated with certain
> religious cults (Lucian *De Dea Syria* 51–2). Castrated slaves were
> not as commonly seen as they were in later centuries, although
> grisly how-to instructions were available in medical texts. We
> may assume that at this time eunuchs with social position were
> practically unknown.[9]

[8]H. J. Lawlor and J. E. L. Oulton, *Eusebius: The Ecclesiastical History and the
Martyrs of Palestine* II (London: SPCK, 1928), 186–87.

[9]Maud W. Gleason, *Making Men: Sophists and Self-presentation in Ancient Rome*
(Princeton: Princeton UP, 1995), 6.

In taking this statement as a starting point for our examination of Melito's *eunouchia* a few refinements may be made. Although there was a traditional association between the cult of Cybele and self-castration, the evidence for such an association in the second century is thin, as it rests entirely on one work of Lucian which is written in a strange Herodotean style. Lucian's *De Dea Syria* is a traveler's tale, a self-conscious work of fiction which provides no evidence of value for the period of its writing. Further, although castrated slaves were perhaps not a daily sight, ample evidence of castrated slaves in the second century is provided by Guyot, including a significant number in Asia.[10] However, it is fair to say that eunuchs with social position were practically unknown. Interestingly the only roughly contemporary congenital eunuch of status she is able to find is Dorotheus, a Christian presbyter at Antioch.[11]

Melito's *eunouchia* has resulted in the suggestion that he was a converted priest of Cybele. But given that the only evidence for such a practice at the time of Melito is that provided by Lucian, this may be safely discounted. Moreover, the manner in which the term is attached to Melito's name would indicate that a trope is in play rather than a physical description. In line with the recognition of the term as a trope, the general interpretation offered is that it means that Melito was celibate. It is a trope however which, given the rhetorical sophistication of Polycrates' writing, may carry more meaning than a first glance might indicate. Quintilian advises a sparing use of metaphor, the function of which is to put things before the eye of the audience in a forceful way.[12] We should thus wonder why Polycrates wishes Victor to know that Melito was celibate, why Melito's *eunouchia* should be put before Victor's eyes in this forceful way, and enquire into the wider net of meaning that the term might have in

---

[10]P. Guyot, *Eunuchen als Sklaven und Freigelassene in der griechisch-Römischen Antike,* Stuttgarter Beiträge zur Geschichte und Politik 14 (Stuttgart: Klett-Cotta, 1980).

[11]Dorotheus, mentioned at Eusebius, *Ecclesiastical History* 7.32.2, cited by Gleason, *Making Men*, 6, n. 23.

[12]Quintilian, *Beginning public speaking* 8.6.19

this context. If Melito, alongside the others, is standing as witness, Polycrates is briefly establishing his credibility, again in keeping with Quintilian's advice. But how, in this case, does *eunouchia* give credibility?

One clue to unpacking the trope may lie in the absence of social status to which Gleason points, for eunuchs in the second century were slaves. This perhaps is the reason why, although celibacy is not unknown in the ancient world outside Christianity, the term *eunouchia* is not used by non-Christian writers, but is employed by Clement and Athenagoras as the male equivalent of virginity. It is possible that Matthew 19.12 lies behind this usage,[13] but Christians who adopt this term, among whom must be counted the author of the first Gospel, are doing more than stating their celibacy, they are deliberately adopting a tone and name indicative of a servile status, indicating something of the manner in which they rejoice in being despised by the world and are absolutely subject to God.

Melito may have been known as the eunuch, but he is a person of high education, and we have seen that he was bishop. As a eunuch Melito nonetheless governs the church; indeed, it is as a eunuch that he governs. He has status not only within the church but without, for given that he is bishop of his church the probability is that he is also a householder, but his real social status is being rhetorically inverted. The servile status is that which the bishop holds towards the God whom he serves; the householder plays the role of eunuch within his own household, which is the household of God. The eunuch is a servant. But a eunuch, whilst naturally a servant, is a servant of a particular kind. To illustrate the particular role of servile eunuchs we may note the significant role played by eunuchs in the *Cyropaedia* of Xenophon. Here they are servants with particular advantages to their master. Because they are cut off from normal family life, they

---

[13]Note the discussion of W. Bauer, "Mt 19:12 und die alten Christen" *Neutestamentliche Studien Georg Heinrici zu seinem 70 Geburtstag dargebracht* (Leipzig: Hinrichs, 1914), 235–244, at 236. Bauer cites Athenagoras, *Plea* 33.34, Clement, *Miscellanies* 3.1.1; 3.1.4, 3.1.91 and *Pedagogue* 3.4.26 as well as Ps-Cyprian, *On Single Clergy* 31.37 and is unsure whether Matthew plays a role in this usage or not.

are the perfect servants and managers; as bodyguards they show a greater bravery than any other because they have nobody they love more than their master, and as objects of contempt they have an even greater loyalty to their master who honors them nonetheless. They are without familial ties, and so their master and their service is their family.[14] This is the role which Melito plays in his own church, which is not his own but God's. But Melito the eunuch is not only a socially inverted yet perfect servant of God, however, for yet more lies behind the statement of Polycrates than that Melito was the ideal bishop because of his commitment in service. The point is the absence of familial ties which Melito professed. Ascetically practiced celibacy is part of this but does not exhaust the meaning, for *eunouchia* took one out of family networks altogether. We have already seen that Melito's embrace of Christ alienated him from his Jewish family. Melito as Jew had cut himself off from his family as a result of his embrace of Christianity and stands as an exemplar of one whose alienation from his own race is complete. As a man of education whose whole service is to the despised Church, he stands as an object of contempt, and yet he is acknowledged by Polycrates as one whose governance of the household of the Church was perfect in the Spirit. Celibacy may have been part of this, though not as an end in itself but as a means by which he could be a yet more perfect servant to his master. Melito as eunuch represents loyalty and devotion displaced from the more usual network of family relationships to the church, and more particularly to its Lord.

Elsewhere Eusebius gives a list of Melito's works and quotes from his *Apology* to the Emperor Marcus Aurelius and from his *Extracts* from the Old Testament, in which Melito gives us his Old Testament canon and tells of a visit to Palestine.[15] Apart from these reports there are but a few inconclusive references in other ancient

---

[14]See especially Xenophon, *Cyropaedia* 7.5.59–65 and the discussion of eunuchs in Xenophon's works by Yun Lee Too, "Xenophon's Cyropaedia: Disfiguring the Pedagogical State," in *Pedagogy and Power: Rhetorics of Classical Learning*, Yun Lee Too and Niall Livingstone, eds. (Cambridge: CUP, 1998), 282–302.

[15]Fragment 3 below, from Eusebius, *Ecclesiastical History* 4.26.

writers, which themselves are chiefly gathered from hints left by
Eusebius. We must, however, deal with a puzzling report concerning *On Pascha* which Eusebius preserves for us: Eusebius purports
to quote from *On Pascha*, but then gives us an introduction which
is not only absent from the work which we possess, but appears to
point to a different work altogether. Further confusion is caused
because Eusebius elsewhere states that Melito wrote "two books on
the Pascha." In preparation for studying this report we should note
how the document translated and presented here was discovered
and the text established.

ON PASCHA

On Pascha was first published in 1940. This edition was based on a
single, fifth century, codex, which the editor, Bonner, had assembled
from two separate collections.[16] Since the colophon was missing,
the work was identified as that of Melito on the basis of the heading
MELEITŌN, on the grounds that its style fulfilled what might have
been expected of Melito's work, and because of its conformity with
Syriac fragments already in existence.[17] Bonner entitled it *On the
Passion* on the basis of a fragment of Anastasius of Sinai.[18] In the
following years further fragments and a Latin epitome were found,
but the most significant discovery was that of a further, almost
complete Greek version in Papyrus Bodmer 13.[19] This was entitled
Of Melito, on Pascha, which suggested that the work was related to
the Quartodeciman paschal celebrations. Finally a Coptic text was
published in 1990.[20]

[16]Campbell Bonner, *The Homily on the Passion by Melito Bishop of Sardis and
Some Fragments of the Apocryphal Ezekiel* (London: Christophers, 1940), 5–8.

[17]Bonner, *Homily,* 7.

[18]Fragment 7 below.

[19]M. Testuz, ed. *Papyrus Bodmer XIII, Méliton de Sardes Homélie sur la Pâque*
(Geneva: Bodmer, 1960).

[20]It may be found in James E. Goehring, *The Crosby Schøyen Codex: MS 193 in
the Schøyen Collection* (Louvain: Peeters, 1990).

Although Bonner's identification of the work he had assembled as that of Melito has received widespread acceptance, there have been a few dissenting voices. The cause of this dissent derives from the report of Melito's work found in Eusebius. This report has been subject to much debate.[21]

> In his work "Concerning the Pascha" he indicates the time at which he drew it up at the beginning, stating thus: When Servillius Paulus was proconsul of Asia, and Sagaris was martyred at a fitting time, there was a great dispute in Laodicea concerning the Pascha, which fell most fittingly in those days. And these things were written:
>
>> Clement the Alexandrian records this matter in his own work concerning the Pascha which he says he composed because of Melito's writing.

Although it is possible that this is a citation from a different work by Melito altogether, since Eusebius records elsewhere that Melito wrote two works on the Pascha, this is not a necessary conclusion. The account of two works might well be the result of another work becoming attached to Melito's *On Pascha*. Eusebius is probably working from a library catalogue and had no direct knowledge of these works. The same is true of the apparent citation from Melito, the chronological note that is reproduced here. The fact that it ends with the words "these things were written" is indicative that what had gone before was not part of the work at all but a chronological note which had been appended to *On Pascha*. Finally, the fact that Clement wrote in response to Melito does not mean that Melito's work was polemical in intent, as might be deduced from the connection with the dispute at Laodicea, even were it possible with certainty to determine what was at issue in the dispute.

The most probable cause of the dispute is the time of day at which to keep the Pascha. It would seem that some Quartodecimans kept

---

[21]Fragment 4 below, from Eusebius, *Ecclesiastical History* 4.26.

the Pascha in the early evening, at the same time as the Jews, whereas others, among whom Melito is probably to be included, postponed the celebration until the time at which the Jewish festivities ended.[22] Both practices were probably ancient, but in time problems were caused because of the difficulty of keeping the Pascha openly in the evening. Because it would be in breach of Roman law it might be seen as inviting martyrdom. A defense on the basis that Jesus kept the Pascha in this manner could be answered with reference to Melito's theory of typology according to which the lamb of the paschal meal was superseded by Christ the true paschal lamb, and that the Jewish festivity likewise was superseded and not to be kept. If Melito's work was in any way connected with this dispute it was probably a secondary involvement of this nature.

The dispute at Laodicea is impossible to date on the basis of the reference to Servillius Paulus since no such figure is known. There are gaps in our knowledge of the proconsular years, and so it is not impossible that there was such a figure, and since the Pauli were major landowners in Asia it is also possible that a member of the family held another, local, office which has been confused with the proconsulate. For this reason, and because the connection with Melito's work is secondary, this chronological note is of no assistance in dating *On Pascha*. More significantly it throws no doubt on the fact that the work which has survived is that of "Melito the eunuch . . . who lies at Sardis."

The text used as the basis of this translation is that of Hall, here reprinted with permission; account is taken of the revisions which Hall has proposed more recently, most of which, however, concern the apparatus.[23] Questions of text are not raised here at all but should be followed through in Hall's critical edition.

[22]So Stewart-Sykes, *Lamb's High Feast*, 155–60, 167–72.
[23]S. G. Hall, "Melito *Peri Pascha:* Corrections and Revisions," *Journal of Theological Studies* 64 (2013): 105–10.

Sardis

Sardis was already an ancient city at the time of Melito. It was strategically situated on what had formerly been the great east-west highway through Asia Minor. At the time of Melito, however, it had been part of the wider Hellenistic world for hundreds of years, and its significance was fundamentally cultural, as a centre of Hellenistic civilization standing alongside the other major cities of Asia. By the time of Melito all trace of the ancient city would have perished as the result of a major earthquake early in the first century. The city was rebuilt, largely from imperial funds. The main Roman street of the city was of marble, running along the east-west axis. It had an elevated pavement and a colonnade of shops on either side. Behind this main street to the north was the gymnasium complex, which was eventually to consist of a pair of halls one hundred meters long with an oiling room. At the time of Melito, however, only the gymnasium proper stood, having been finished about AD 166. Between the gymnasium and the main street was a thriving bazaar area, including a Jewish section. This centre was situated near the Pacteolus, on the east bank, and to the north of the city, while settlement extended to the south and east, up the hillside and away from the valley itself.

Apart from its cultural significance and the presence of Melito, Sardis is of interest to students of early Christianity because it is one of the churches addressed by the seer of Revelation, and because it is also a centre of Jewish civilization in Asia. In particular, a vast synagogue has been unearthed at Sardis, certainly the largest and perhaps the richest Roman synagogue to have been discovered. Melito exhibits a great deal of anti-Jewish sentiment, and it has often been suggested that this is the result of the differing social situation of the Christians and the Jews. This may be so, but the synagogue cannot be used to support such a claim, as it certainly was not built as a synagogue but as a public building and was taken over for use as a synagogue only in the fourth century.

Judaism and Christianity were not the only religions at Sardis in the period. Among other religions, most notable is the cult of Artemis, the civic cult. To her was dedicated the large Hellenistic temple by the Pacteolus. She appears to have taken on some of the appurtenances of the native Cybele. The worship of Sabazios was also common in Sardis, but he appears to have been identified with Zeus and also with the god of the Jews; apart from Sabazios the numismatic evidence indicates that Herakles and Dionysus were also worshipped. Also significant was the imperial cultus; Sardis competed with ten other Asian cities to be the home of a temple to Tiberius and pleaded its case before the Senate. The evidence of visits from both Marcus Aurelius and Verus, who for a time was co-emperor with Marcus Aurelius, is an indication that imperial loyalty continued to run high in the time of Melito.

MELITO THE SOPHIST

In the second century, rhetoric, an ancient and essential skill for politicians and lawyers, had grown out of these narrow confines and become something akin to a spectator sport. Aristotle had defined rhetoric as being either dicanic, related to the law court, and political or persuasive, or epideictic, a branch of oratory meant to confirm an audience in opinions which it already held.[24] These modes of rhetoric were all practiced as part of the education of a wealthy man in the ancient world, and the practice of the schools, especially in epideictic oratory, which lent itself readily to display, had become more widespread. Orators could become wealthy and enjoy great popular success. At the same time a particular style of oratory had developed which was known as the Asianist style. As opposed to the Attic style, which sought to use only the vocabulary and forms of the classic Athenian orators, the Asianist style tended to be flowery, almost poetic, and innovative in its vocabulary. Melito's rhetoric is clearly that of the Asianist school, and we may deduce that he had

[24]Aristotle, *Rhetoric* 1.3–1.9.

received a rhetorical education. On this basis we have sought to observe a number of classical parallels in *On Pascha*. His adoption of rhetoric was only natural when he came to speak of the Pascha, for it was common for religious festivals to be the occasion of rhetoric and hymnic prose.

We may note a number of rhetorical devices in Melito's work. It is impossible to render them all in translation, but opportunity has been taken to reproduce something of Melito's style. Among rhetorical devices we may note:

- *Homoioteleuton* (lines ending in the same way): see *On Pascha* 93.

- *Homoiarcton* (a series of lines beginning in the same way): see *On Pascha* 73.

- *Paronomasia in antithesis* (wordplay intended to point up a contrast): the translator has contrived to create an example at *On Pascha* 53, though this is not in the original. For an example in the Greek, see *On Pascha* 21.

- *Address to persons and objects not present*: See the address to the angel at *On Pascha* 32.

- *Asyndeton* (lists not joined together with conjunctions): see the vice list at *On Pascha* 50.

Observing Melito's rhetoric, however, goes beyond noticing individual elements in the speech, because a knowledge of the rhetorical canons of his age enables us to interpret the work as a whole. In the first instance we should note not only that there is great similarity in the forms of speech employed by Melito and those used by contemporary orators, but we should also note that rhetoric was bound up closely to religions functions in the Roman Empire. The speeches which preserve for us the most ornate style, including strings of special attributes like that which we can see at *On Pascha* 82, are prose hymns composed on various occasions in honor of the gods of the empire. Polemo, perhaps the most famous and successful orator of Melito's time, famously dedicated the Temple of Olympian Zeus in the presence of the Emperor Hadrian through a hymn, composed as a speech, and delivered, he claimed, under divine inspiration.[25] We may therefore, in view of the style of *On Pascha*, determine that Melito is presenting us not with a sermon as is widely held by Protestant commentators, but with a liturgical text, a speech which accompanies and effects a liturgical event. Thus observations of similarities between Jewish hymns, and Byzantine Holy Week hymns,[26] even if they do not prove a shared history or direct dependence, do show that the setting and context are the same.

In addition to seeing the context in which *On Pascha* might be delivered, the study of rhetoric allows us to see how the prose-hymn might fit into the liturgical action of the Quartodecimans. Every speech had the same basic shape. There might be other elements, and the elements might vary in significance according to the occasion of the speech, but nonetheless the same basic template can be laid out.

- *Propositio/thesis*: Here the orator sets out in brief what the speech will achieve.

- *Narratio/diēgēma*: Here the orator tells a story. In the case of a courtroom speech it might be the facts of the case, or else the background to the occasion. On a religious occasion a story relating to the god being praised, or to the feast, might be told.

- *Probatio/kataskeuē*: Here the case is proved. The *diēgēma* is shown to be true (or false!). In a courtroom speech the weight might well be found in this part of the speech.

[25]Philostratus, *Lives of the Sophists* 1.533.

[26]Note, in addition to those cited in the bibliography, Panagiotos Chrestos, "Τὸ ἔργον τοῦ Μελίτωνος Περὶ Πάσχα καὶ ἡ ἀκολουθία τοῦ πάθους," *Kleronomia* 1 (1969): 65–78.

- *Peroratio/epilogos*: Here the orator sums up, ensuring the audience is on his side, and bringing about in the audience an emotional response proper to the occasion.

On Pascha follows this outline. Melito himself points out the transitions from *propositio* to *narratio* and from *narratio* to *probatio*, and these divisions are moreover marked off by doxologies. This observation allows us to recognize the transition from *probatio* to *peroratio*, since here also there is a doxology. In the first part of the speech he sets out the fundamental themes of the Pascha, the slaughter of the sheep and the life of the Lord. In the second part he retells the story of the Egyptian passover, at first staying quite close to the scriptural text and then going on to a graphic description of the slaughter of the firstborn intended, as Greek writers on oratory suggested, to bring home an emotional response in his audience as he presents the picture. His *probatio* then sets the story in a wider perspective, that of the fall of Adam and the redemption wrought by Christ. Finally, in conclusion he brings the blame on Israel and demonstrates nonetheless the triumph of Christ. It should be noted however that in this section the guilt of Israel is played out as a counterpoint to the praise of the acts of God in redemption both under the new and the old covenants. The end of the speech finds the risen Christ present in the person and the voice of Melito, inviting the Gentiles to forgiveness and to salvation.

The exceptional element to this pattern is the discussion of typology which occurs after the *narratio*. However, ancient rhetoricians were often prone to digress, and handbooks advise such a procedure. The intention was to maintain the interest of the audience by digressing in such a way that the overall interest of the speech is served. Melito does this by reflecting on the manner in which the Pascha is the fulfillment of prophecy and at the same time the fulfillment in the Lord's Pascha is the annulment of the former rite.

The pattern of *On Pascha* is thus the normal pattern of a speech. But Melito has bound this pattern to the liturgical action of the

Quartodeciman Pascha, as we may see after a brief review of the paschal liturgy as Melito would have known it.

THE QUARTODECIMAN LITURGY AND
MELITO'S *ON PASCHA*[27]

The Quartodeciman Pascha comprised what we would know both as Good Friday and as Easter, for in keeping with the Johannine tradition according to which the crucifixion was itself the manifestation of God's glory, and in keeping with the Jewish liturgical tradition of a single celebration of the Passover, the Pascha was a single festival which commemorated both the passion and the resurrection. Thus at the end of *On Pascha*, even as the events of the crucifixion are being described in counterpoint to the celebrations of the Jews, the risen Lord appears and announces his triumph.

The Quartodeciman paschal liturgy can be reconstructed as follows:

The Fast

Given that the Jewish tradition had been to keep a fast before the Passover, it is only natural that Quartodecimans should continue this tradition. Jews fasted from the time of the evening sacrifice, and the probability is that this was the original Quartodeciman practice. As the two religions formed, the original justification was forgotten. Three reasons are variously given for fasting practice:

- To share in the sufferings of the Lord.

- To fast on behalf of the Jews during their feasting.

- To prepare oneself to receive Communion at the paschal feast.

---

[27]For detail on all that follows below and for bibliography see *The Lamb's High Feast*, 142–206.

All of these are probably secondary, and need not be mutually exclusive. Melito contrasts the sufferings of the Lord with the celebrations of the Jews, and this is certainly an indication that he is fasting at the time the Jews are keeping their celebration. This celebration concluded at midnight, so it is reasonable to deduce that this was the time at which the Quartodecimans began their celebration, but that they gathered at the time at which they would once have gathered for Passover, namely around sundown on the fourteenth Nisan. The rationale for his fasting is probably the first, though there is also some possibility that this melds in with the second justification. This does not help us determine the point at which the fast began. Irenaeus says that there is a variety of times for which the fast is kept, and beyond this we probably cannot go. Much greater problems were caused by variation in the time at which the fast concluded: it appears that some Quartodecimans concluded the fast and began their celebration at the onset of night, the time at which the Jews likewise began their celebration, at which time other Quartodecimans would be fasting, and perhaps gathering to keep a vigil. It seems most probable, from the manner in which Melito contrasts the sufferings of the Lord with the celebrations of the Jews, that he kept a vigil for the first part of the night and that the celebration began around midnight.

The Vigil

All that can be known for certain about the vigil of the Quartodecimans is that Exodus 12 was read, as Melito tells us, and that some discussion and exposition of that reading, as found in *On Pascha*, followed. On this basis we may see the first part of *On Pascha* as the material employed by Melito in keeping this part of the vigil. We may also suggest that there was a strong eschatological tone to the night of waiting, in that just as Jews looked forward to the coming of the Messiah on the Passover night, so Christians likewise not only perceived that the Messiah came to them in the celebration and commemoration of the Pascha but believed that this might be the occasion of the Lord's final return. In a later period there is some indication that the parable of the wise and foolish virgins was read and expounded, which is further indication of the eschatological tone of the vigil. Finally, there is a strong possibility that there were readings from the Old Testament prophets. This was certainly the case in Syria, as can be seen from the vigil described in the *Didascalia* which clearly derived from the same roots as that known to Melito.[28] The reading of prophecies from the Old Testament would accord with the eschatological tone of the vigil and fit in with Melito's numerous citations from the prophets.

The Celebration

Around midnight the fast was broken and the celebration, including the commemoration of the triumph of Christ amid his sufferings, would begin. *On Pascha* commemorates precisely this, and we may see that this would have accompanied the table rite as a declaration of God's mighty works in a transformation of customs of reading, discussing, and singing found within the Graeco-Roman symposium.

I Hors d'oeuvres
    First cup of wine

II Main course (bread served at this point)
    Second cup of wine
    Meal
    Third cup of wine

This was the shape of any formal meal in the ancient world, with the omission of a dessert. This was replaced by the final piece of bread known as the *aphikoman*, a piece broken off from the main loaf at the beginning of the meal and hidden only to be re-introduced at the conclusion of the meal. The probability is that this was originally intended to represent the presence of the Messiah. Melito

---

[28]*Didascalia* 21. See the selection from this chapter at p. 116 below.

uses the word *aphikomenos* (coming one) suddenly at the beginning of the fourth part of *On Pascha*, and we may therefore deduce that this is the moment at which the meal concluded, after the hearing of the basic haggadah which constitutes the third part, and the time at which the Messiah was perceived to have come in the presence of the bread. In other words, the whole of *On Pascha* is intended to commemorate and to make present the work of God, the whole is a commemoration, and as such its intent was sacramental. The *aphikoman* could be received in the presence of the risen Jesus, as the voice of the risen Jesus could be heard speaking through Melito as he declaimed: "I am the Passover of your salvation." And so the risen Jesus could be known in the sharing of the broken bread.

After this a third cup is permissible, and if the early Christians were anything like the Jews, and anything like modern Christians, it is far from impossible that a further cup (or two!) might be added, and that the celebration might continue until the dawn of the following day.

In conclusion we may understand the outline of *On Pascha* as follows:

- *Propositio*: The Scripture has been read, and in the paschal celebration we can come to realize how it is fulfilled.

- *Narratio*: The firstborn of the Egyptians died horribly whilst Israel was liberated. The liberation of Israel is the experience of the Christian through the commemoration of the death of Christ.

- *Probatio*: The whole was the result of Adam's disgrace, as we remember the history of humankind in need of salvation.

- *Peroratio:* Yet the Messiah came, and comes to us. In the murder of Christ by Israel, repeating their slaughter of the lamb, is the triumph of God, which in its proclamation is a present reality for us as we celebrate.

On Pascha is itself the text of the liturgy, the means by which the Christians of Sardis, gathered with Melito their bishop, might commemorate and know the presence of Jesus in his triumph.

It may however seem puzzling that there is no eucharistic prayer as such, no direct reference to gifts of bread and wine (the references are there, but indirect), no epiclesis (for all that Melito assumes the activity of the Spirit he does not have a pneumatology as such, as we shall see later in this introduction) and certainly no reference to the Last Supper. But were Melito to point to the Last Supper he would have been stepping out of his Johannine tradition; there were indeed Quartodecimans who saw the Last Supper as the fulfillment of the Pascha,[29] but Melito was not among them. For him the death of the Lord at the same time as, and in place of, the death of the Passover lambs was the fulfillment of the Pascha. There are a number of early prayers for the Eucharist or for related table rites which take no account of the Last Supper, and Melito's work can stand among them. Certainly it is also (in part at least) a prophetic homily, but the words of Enrico Mazza concerning another description of early Christian worship (Acts 20.9–11) may stand here:

> Paul's words were not just what we could call a homily. It was the liturgical celebration itself, including at the same time liturgical text, proclamation, comment, homily, and physical action, all of which, lasting till dawn, had the characteristics of a vigil.[30]

In time this proclamation of God's mighty acts as a means of making them present entered into the eucharistic tradition and is still to be found in liturgies both eastern and western, in the declaration of God's deeds at the beginning of every eucharistic prayer.

---

[29]See the citation from Hippolytus, taken from the *Chronicon Paschale*, at p. 107 below.

[30]Enrico Mazza, *The Origins of the Eucharistic Prayer* (Collegeville, MN: Liturgical Press, 1995), 105.

THE QUARTODECIMAN PASCHA AND THE JEWISH PESAH

The reconstruction attempted here, based on the detailed treatment to be found in *The Lamb's High Feast,* depends in part on the assumption that the liturgy of the Quartodecimans followed the broad outlines of the Jewish rite. However, our knowledge of Jewish Passover ritual at the time is sketchy. The basic document for constructing the liturgy of the Jewish Passover at the time of Melito, or more accurately for the period before that of Melito since his liturgy would be formed as much by Christian tradition as by direct Jewish influence, is the Tractate of the Mishnah known as *Pesahim*, which is from a later period than that of Melito; also to be taken into account is the Tosefta tractate of the same name. These, however, display significant differences from each other, particularly in the topic of discussion over the meal. In view of the lateness of this evidence recent scholars have argued that the derivation of a paschal rite from *Peri Pascha* on the basis of a Jewish foundation is illegitimate.[31] However, I will argue, albeit briefly, that we have sufficient information to proceed legitimately to ground Melito's paschal practice in his Jewish heritage.

In the first instance we may be sure that domestic liturgies occurred alongside the Temple liturgy of the slaughter of the Passover lambs. In the diaspora Philo describes the manner in which, at the Passover, every house is dressed as a temple, as well as the festal meal of the occasion, in which ancestral customs are fulfilled with prayers and hymns.[32] And we may also note the domestic extension of the Passover within Jerusalem presupposed by the Last Supper narratives of the synoptic Gospels. With the destruction of the Temple there is a renewed focus on the domestic setting of the Passover, and it is this which is legislated by the Mishnah. Of course the Mishnah does not describe every event, but we should recall that what is common is often passed over in silence in ancient sources.

[31]So, in particular, Joshua Kulp, "The Origins of the Seder and Haggadah," *Currents in Biblical Research* 4 (2005): 109–34.

[32]*Special laws* 2.148–9.

However, when we read of the statement of Gamaliel that the Passover, the unleavened bread, and the bitter herbs should be mentioned in the course of the meal, in following Bokser by finding that mention of the Passover substitutes for the absence of the lamb,[33] we may also suggest that these are traditional foods for the paschal table. Thus Kulp summarizes the current scholarly consensus as "there was no seder or haggadah while the Temple still stood,"[34] a consensus with which he apparently agrees, yet accepts that there was a gathering and a meal at which, alongside the paschal lamb, bitter herbs and unleavened bread were eaten, wine was drunk, and psalms were sung.[35] Thus the Mishnah reports the transformation of a rite already in existence rather than creating an entirely new one, a rite which had to undergo some transformation as a result of the destruction of the Temple, but which at the same time required some conformity with the prior ritual.

As such we may conclude that Passover was marked by a domestic meal ritual. We may also suggest, without reference to the Mishnah, that hymns were sung and Scripture read and discussed, in part on the basis of the reports in Philo and in the Gospels, and in part on the basis that this would be expected at any festal gathering; we may be clear that for Jews and Christians alike this gathering was a species of the common Graeco-Roman symposium.[36] Thus when there are clear parallels between the practice of *Peri Pascha* and Jewish Passover practice as it later emerged, then these can hardly be coincidental. Thus there is a close verbal correspondence between Mishnah *Pesahim* 10.5, which appears in the (later) Passover haggadah, and *On Pascha* 68. Similarly, we may observe the use of the term *aphikomenos* of Christ at *On Pascha* 66 and 86; at these points it is used of Christ in respect of his coming to earth to heal

[33]Baruch M. Bokser, *The Origins of the Seder: The Passover Rite and Early Rabbinic Judaism* (Berkeley: University of California, 1984), 42, 44.

[34]Kulp, "Origins," 110.

[35]Kulp, "Origins," 112–3.

[36]So, also, Jordan D. Rosenblum, *Food and Identity in Early Rabbinic Judaism* (Cambridge: CUP, 2010), 169.

the suffering. This is significant because it reflects the *aphikoman* of the Jewish Passover rite, a rite which was arguably originally messianic in its significance.[37] Finally we should note that, according to the Mishnah, the discussion of God's mighty acts should "begin with the disgrace and end with the glory";[38] this is the shape of the second part of *On Pascha*, which begins with Adam's fall and ends with Christ's triumph.

The question of whether the exodus was a set topic for discussion is less certain, and we may well anticipate a degree of variety within forming Jewish practice, as in forming Christian practice; although there is no evidence of discussion of Exodus 12 in extant Jewish sources, there is such uncertainty that it is not inconceivable that Melito found this in the tradition, though it is equally possible that the choice of reading Exodus 12 in the context of a vigil was his. To discuss the date and genesis of the Mishnaic discussion of the details of Pesah would take us beyond the point of the present discussion; it is sufficient to agree that there are significant and suggestive parallels between the Mishnaic arrangements for a festal symposium and *Peri Pascha*, as well as significant differences. For Melito, as for the compilers of the Mishnah, Pesah/Pascha was a time at which, in the context of a nocturnal meal, extra-familial groups would gather to celebrate and to reflect upon the liberation which they had experienced.[39] It is therefore entirely legitimate to understand *On Pascha* against a background of developing understandings of Pascha/Pesah and developing expressions within both Judaism and Christianity.

This then allows us to fit the work in with information gathered from elsewhere[40] to give us a clear picture of the celebration known to Melito, the task undertaken above, as a gathering for reading and

---

[37] Notably Mishnah *Pesahim* forbids the ritual of *aphikoman*.

[38] Mishnah *Pesahim* 10.4.

[39] For this note particularly the summary of Duval's modern Hebrew article in Igor Dorfmann-Lazarev, "La 'Pâque d'Égypte' et la 'Pâque de Jérusalem': l'herméneutique de l'Exode dans les traditions chrétienne et rabbinique selon I. Y. Duval," *Istina* 48 (2003): 359–73.

[40] Such as the Syrian *Didascalia* and the *Epistula Apostolorum*. The sources are all to be found in translation in this book.

discussion of Scripture moves to the eating of a joyous meal, and concludes with the singing of hymns. The discussion of Exodus 12 within *On Pascha* thus corresponds to the first part of this celebration, the central proof of the narrative to the hinge of the celebration as the resurrection is recognized, and the joyous conclusion to the singing of hymns in a paschal context.

One question, however, is the legitimacy of referring to any of this as a haggadah. Recent research indicates that the formation of the paschal haggadah as presently known is significantly later than once argued;[41] as such it is hard to see any influence on the paschal rite of Quartodecimans. Insofar as the paschal haggadah is a fixed midrash, and does not relate to Exodus 12, no relationship is to be sought in any case; insofar as the term haggadah loosely means a retelling, or proclamation, and insofar as the present fixed form may have derived from earlier extempore productions from within a sympotic setting, then it may well be argued that *Peri Pascha* is precisely such a production, and that its genesis lies in the same social and cultural matrix which formed paschal haggadah in forming Jewish circles, of which the haggadah at present extant is a descendant. However, to avoid misunderstanding, perhaps the term should be avoided.[42]

I will, nonetheless, assert that the Quartodeciman gathering is indeed an outgrowth from Jewish practice. To this compare the conclusions of Leonard: "There is no indication that the liturgical form or theological contents of the Quartodeciman Pascha *continued* a form of the Jewish Pesah as it is built structurally *against* a celebration of the Pesah that lasted some time into the night. The Quartodecimans' liturgies require fasting, praying and mourning 'for' the Jews."[43] Here we have a false dichotomy. Apart from the issue

[41]See in particular Clemens Leonhard, *The Jewish Pesach and the Origins of the Christian Easter* (Berlin: de Gruyter, 2006), 73–118.

[42]In this respect some of the argument in *The Lamb's High Feast* might be revised; however, as may already be clear, in the reconstruction of the Quartodeciman Pascha and its correlation with *Peri Pascha* I suggest that the argument is still sound.

[43]Leonhard, *Jewish Pesach,* 305; italics original.

that overmuch weight is given to the explanation of the paschal fast as a vicarious fast for the Jews, whereas this is just one justification which is offered and is probably secondary, there is no reason why the practice of a paschal symposium might not have been inherited by Christians of Jewish descent and practice, and subsequently adjusted (particularly with regard to the timing of the fast and of the breaking of the fast, which varied among Quartodeciman groups) in order to put distance between themselves as a forming religion and those who, by the middle of the second century, are distinctly and independently Jewish.

Melito's anti-Judaism[44]

To our ears Melito's attitude to the Jews is horrifying. In hearing what he has to say we should recall that Jews probably outnumbered Christians in Sardis, and that Melito himself was of Jewish stock.

A number of factors come into play when Melito deals with Judaism, but two factors in particular are predominant. First of all, we should note that Melito is a Christian standing in the Johannine tradition. We may note here the consistent anti-Judaism of *John*, a Gospel that is also firmly engaged with Jewish practice: "John is both Jewish and anti-Jewish."[45] The points made by John are substantially those of Melito; for Melito, as for John, Christ has superseded the law (Jn 10.34, 15.25; cf. *On Pascha* 7, 40–3). The Jews do not listen to Jesus, nor do they see God in him, whereas the Johannine community does so (so Jn 1.10–2; 1 Jn 1.1; Jn 9.35–41, and perhaps Jn 1.45–51; cf. *On Pascha* 82). The Jews persecute Jesus, and at the last they execute him (Jn 5.16, 7.1, 8.59; cf. *On Pascha* 92–3, 96). Both moreover are critical of the Temple, another point at which there is distance between Johannine Christianity and Judaism (Jn 2.19–20, 4.21–3; cf. *On Pascha* 45). John's attempt to shift the blame for the

---

[44]For more detail on this subject see the works cited in the bibliography below.
[45]C. K. Barrett, *The Gospel of John and Judaism* (London: SPCK, 1975), 71. John's anti-Judaism has not gone unnoticed before or since.

crucifixion away from the Romans is brought to an apogee in Melito where they do not appear at all. It is not Melito but John who is the first to make the charge of deicide against the Jewish people.[46] The most recent treatment of this issue concludes that the attitude of the Johannine Jews towards Jesus is transparent of the attitude felt by John.[47] Essentially it reflects an argument between an emerging form of Judaism (Johannine Christianity) and representatives of what would become mainstream Judaism. The same remains true of Melito's day and situation.

The problem is made more acute by Melito's Quartodecimanism; just as the Quartodecimans at the time of Nicaea were known as Judaizers, so there is a need for Melito's congregation to distinguish itself from the Jews, practicing a similar rite on the same day, albeit apparently at a different time. Just as the Jews were no longer a people, so their Passover was vacuous of meaning now that the true lamb had been slain. John and Melito must distance themselves from the Jewish community precisely because of the proximity of their religious practice. Like Melito, John has a paschal practice close to that of the Jews, and so at John 2.13 and 6.4 Pascha is specifically described as being that "of the Jews"; that is to say it is distinguished from the Pascha of the Johannine community. The same attitude can be found in the Syrian community producing the *Didascalia*, who are so concerned that their Pascha might be identified with that of the Jews that they actually pray for the annihilation of the Jewish people! On the Jewish side moreover there appears to have been some attempt to put distance between themselves and Quartodeciman Christians. In particular Nodet and Taylor point to the discussion at Mishnah *Pesahim* 7.1–2 as indicating an attempt to avoid the paschal lamb being roasted in the shape of a cross.[48]

---

[46]The phrase of E. Werner, "Melito of Sardes, First Poet of Deicide," *Hebrew Union College Annual* 37 (1966): 191–210.

[47]John Ashton, *Understanding the Fourth Gospel* (Oxford: Clarendon, 1991), 131–59.

[48]Étienne Nodet and Justin Taylor, *The Origins of Christianity: An Exploration* (Collegeville, MN: Liturgical Press, 1998), 352–53.

The Theology of Melito

Because *On Pascha* is a liturgical document its interest is primarily liturgical. However, a number of other aspects of Melito's thought have been discussed since the discovery of this document.

a) Melito's doctrine of God in Christ

Although Origen tells us that Melito thought that God was corporeal, which may be an indication that, like Tertullian, Melito was a stoic,[49] a liturgical and commemorative work like *On Pascha* does not present us with a doctrine of God as such, but rather God is described through his mighty acts of creation and salvation. For Melito, these acts are expressed through Christ made flesh, and Melito's doctrine of Christ as God embodied may be the basis for Origen's claim. We cannot separate Melito's idea of God from his Christology which, as an anonymous third century writer has it, proclaims Christ as both God and man.[50]

Bonner, the first editor of *On Pascha*, characterized Melito's Christology as essentially a pneumatic Christology, and more precisely as a "naive modalism."[51] In other words Bonner felt that Melito did not make a clear distinction between the persons of the Trinity and thought that Melito believed that Christ was empowered by the Holy Spirit. This was a common idea in the second century, but it is not that of Melito. Melito sees Christ as the Creator clothed in flesh. So at *On Pascha* 66, 86 it is the Creator who comes down from heaven, and at *On Pascha* 70 he is enfleshed. *On Pascha* 47, 66 state that the Lord put on humanity as a garment. Although this is clearly defective by the standards of later centuries, it is orthodox within the context of the second century in that Melito is maintaining the

---

[49]This would not be impossible; Melito's treatment of Scripture is reminiscent of the manner in which the stoics discussed ancient literary material. See *The Lamb's High Feast,* 84–92.

[50]See Hall, *Melito on Pascha,* xii with reference to Eusebius, *Ecclesiastical History* 5.28.

[51]Bonner, *Homily,* 28.

fundamental truths that Jesus Christ was God and that he was flesh.
So although Melito's Christology may thus conceivably be described
as modalist, this is not a very helpful definition. His Trinitarian
theology concentrates on the relationship between the Father and
the Son. This is characterized by Hall as "christocentric monotheism"; by this Hall means that for Melito, Christ is God and God is
Christ.[52] There is no real distinction between the Father and the Son,
indeed at one point we read that Christ, "Insofar as he begets, he is
father, insofar as he is begotten, he is Son." Although there has been
an attempt to interpret this passage as referring to the sons whom
Christ begets in salvation, thinking to rescue Melito from any impu-
tation of heresy, elsewhere we hear that "he bears the Father and is
borne by him." However strange this may seem to our ears, in the
context of the second century this is not heretical. By contrast the
Spirit has a limited role to play in *On Pascha*. The Spirit is mentioned
four times, at sections 16, 32, 44, and 66; these references are to the
immortality of the Spirit, which thus protects the Israelite firstborn
as a type in the blood, and as the means by which Christ is able to
conquer death. We must remember that Melito bears witness to the
truth as it was understood in his day and that the Church has grown
gradually in understanding the orthodox faith. At the center of the
Christian faith stands Christ, and Christ is at the center of the faith
proclaimed, lived, and celebrated by Melito.

We should also recollect that this Christology is motivated by
soteriological concerns. The image of God in humanity is impris-
oned in Hades[53] and is rescued by God in humanity. The impulse
for God's act in Christ is the condition of the human creation. It is
for this reason that "the paschal mystery [is] completed in the body
of the Lord."[54]

---

[52]S. G. Hall, "The Christology of Melito: A Misrepresentation Exposed," *Studia
Patristica* 13 (1975): 154–68.
[53]*On Pascha* 55.
[54]*On Pascha* 56.

b) Eschatology

Eschatology for Melito as we may understand him through *On Pascha* is bound up to the liturgical commemoration of the acts of God, through which God in Christ becomes present in mind, in prophetic speech, and through the sacramental agency of the *aphikoman*. The Quartodeciman paschal fast has an eschatological element, not simply a future element, but as related to the meeting of the risen Lord in the assembly. Other Quartodeciman documents such as *Epistula Apostolorum*, and indeed the letter of Polycrates, seem to have a much more futuristic eschatology, and for this reason either Melito or the other Quartodeciman documents have been deemed not Quartodeciman. But the difference is more perceived than real, for although there are differences of emphasis, both point to a lively belief in the revelation of the Messiah in the paschal context. Asia, through its reading of the Apocalypse alongside the fourth Gospel, was an effective incubator for an eschatological hope, but it is not impossible that Asian Christianity sustained a lively futuristic eschatological hope whilst recognizing that the signs of the parousia of Christ were already present. This tension is present in the fourth Gospel and is manifest in the statement that "the hour is coming, and now is, when true worshippers shall worship the Father in spirit and in truth."[55] The realized eschatology which is most prominent in *On Pascha* reflects its liturgical origin,[56] but this is not to say that Melito would not have been conscious of a futuristic element also.

A sidelong glance at Quartodeciman eschatology may be provided in Polycrates' statement that Melito is lying at Sardis and awaiting the visitation (*episkopē*) from the heavens. When Polemo, the famous sophist, was dying, and knew moreover that he was

[55] Jn 4.23.
[56] Thus also Dragoş-Andrei Giulea, *Pre-Nicene Christology in Paschal Contexts: The Case of the Divine Noetic Anthropos* (Leiden: Brill, 2014), 112: "Attending the pascal liturgy involves more than simply prayer and commemoration. It also engages the participant in a process of discovering the Logos-Christ in his manifestation. . . ."

dying, he directed that he should be interred alive, so that he should
not be found silent. As he was walled up his voice cried out that he
should declaim again if he were only to be given a body.[57] Declamation for Polemo was more than a livelihood, it was a life, and the
point of life was to declaim. It is in this light that we should understand Polycrates' statement about Melito, who in the resurrection
will find fulfillment of his own *episkopē*, rather than the empty hope
of Polemo to have a body in order to declaim once again.

c) Typology

In *On Pascha* Melito presents us with an exegetical method which
may be termed "historical typology": the events of the Old Testament are seen to be typified in the New Testament, and there is a
correlation seen between the Old Testament events of liberation and
the New Testament events of salvation. The events of Exodus are
described as types (*typoi*), a word which is also employed by Justin
and Barnabas, although there are certainly differences between
Melito's use of the term and that of his contemporaries. The word
appears in the Pauline correspondence, but the theory itself as presented by Melito has more in common with John than with Paul.
Melito has a theory of typology according to which the type, say the
first Passover, precedes the reality, the salvation worked by Jesus,
which fulfils it. A very similar typological scheme may be seen at
work in the fourth Gospel; for instance, the descent of the manna
given to the Israelites in the wilderness is a type of Christ's descent
as a gift of salvation. In John the law had grace in itself; the grace
brought by Christ may be such as to outweigh it, and in outweighing
to invalidate it, but this does not mean that it had not validity on its
own. In this context we may note the intrusion of "true" (*alēthinos*)
in John 6.32; this is reflected by the word which Melito employs to
describe the reality as opposed to the type, *alētheia*. Whereas the
law was given by Moses, grace and truth came through Jesus Christ.
Both the thought and the language here are as much Melito's as they

[57]Philostratus, *Lives of the Sophists* 1.544.

are John's.[58] According to Melito's theory the types are temporary in effect. Thus the blood of the paschal lamb is a type, or prefiguration, of the blood of Christ, as is the law of the gospel. The sufferings of the just, like Abel and Joseph, are types of the sufferings of Christ.[59] Melito compares these types to sculptors' working models and to metaphors; they are of use only until the finished work has been made. The people of Israel are as the artist's model, a preliminary sketch for the Church. The law is the metaphor by which the gospel is elucidated.[60]

But apart from its Johannine roots, Melito's theory of typology may also owe something to a common fund of philosophical wisdom. The process by which events in history occur beforehand as types which are ultimately fulfilled, so making it possible for the event to be interpreted in the light of the prefiguration, leads Melito to state that there are specific and proper times for each stage of this process. The extended image of the preliminary sketch is taken from sculpture, but this may be a pedagogic explanation of an interpretative theory which has already come to him in a developed form. This view is not, however, explicit in Melito. Melito's philosophical knowledge is that of the stoic interpreter of Homer. In the time of Melito the subject of allegorization both of ancient religious myth and of poetry was a live one. May we not see Melito's typological system in this context, as a response to the debate about the value and function of allegorical interpretation in the rhetorical schools? Not, of course, that his theory is identical to any of those produced by the pagan thinkers, but that he sees himself in a similar context, both in interpreting an authoritative text and in interpreting its religious content. It is highly unlikely that Melito in Sardis could have been unaware of the debate. He would naturally read the Scripture in the way in which Cornutus, the stoic interpreter of Homeric myth, read the poets, as a riddle which hides a wisdom.

[58]So compare *On Pascha* 7 with Jn 1.17.
[59]*On Pascha* 59.
[60]*On Pascha* 40.

The wisdom, for Melito, would be the eternal wisdom of God. The typological method would be the means by which the riddle is understood. Apart, however, from Melito's use of the image of the sculptors' working models,[61] there is a significant difference between Melito and his pagan contemporaries in their attitudes to history. Whereas the pagans differed in the extent to which they would consider the events described to be historical, this consideration was not of central relevance to their treatments of the texts. On the whole the literal meaning is to be altogether rejected. This is certainly true of Heraclitus, to an extent of Plutarch, and apparently the meaning of Cornutus and of Maximus of Tyre (although this is not explicitly stated),[62] whereas for Melito the significance of the events he describes inheres in their historical character. Had they not taken place then his theory of typology would not be possible. The literal meaning is no longer significant, but it is not simply a construction to hide a greater intended significance. The metaphor is understood in the light of the gospel which is the reality to which the metaphor points, but the metaphor must retain its own literal and historical significance in order to be an effective metaphor pointing to a greater reality. This is in line with the argument of Quintilian that historical narratives are to be preferred to those which are fictitious or merely realistic, since the force of such a narrative is in proportion to its truth.[63] Melito is thus a clear example of a practitioner of a typology in which the place of history is significant, and in this lies a significant difference between Melito's treatment of his authoritative text and that of his pagan contemporaries. In essence, however, he is doing much the same as his contemporaries whilst at the same time differentiating himself from them, in much the same way that he is liturgically acting in a way much like that of the Jews whilst putting distance between himself and them.

[61]Quintilian frequently employs the image of the sculptor and the statue for the construction of a speech by an orator, but does not make use of the idea of working models.

[62]See *The Lamb's High Feast,* 84–92.

[63]Quintilian, *Beginning public speaking* 2.4.2.

Conclusion: Melito's liturgical theology

Although Melito himself would not think in the categories in which we think, we can justly understand him from within the framework of liturgical theology. *On Pascha* is a liturgical document, and in the light of the Jewish understanding of remembrance as a means of making the past a present reality, and bringing to bear the blessings of the past in the hope of the future, as in the light of Hellenistic theories about the way in which rhetoric might bring to life in the minds and ears of the audience a reality not present, we may understand that for Melito and for his hearers the liturgy was the point at which the glory of God in Jesus Christ, the resurrection triumph and the pains of the passion, the proclamation of the Scriptures and the experience of salvation now and in the future came to life and reality. In proclamation both of scriptural past and prophetic present,[64] in the presence of Christ in the sacramentally transformed rite of *aphikoman* and in his prophetic voice, in the experience of rejoicing after vigil and fasting, in the light suffusing the paschal night from full moon and kindled lamps, Melito and his congregation met their Lord and were enabled to proclaim his eternal triumph in an eternal commemoration.

Further Reading

This short bibliography is restricted to works in English. Other works are cited in the footnotes, and further bibliography can be found in *The Lamb's High Feast*.

Melito and Peri Pascha

Hall, S. G. *Melito of Sardis: On Pascha and Fragments.* Oxford: Clarendon, 1979.

---

[64]On this see now Dragoş-Andrei Giulea, "Seeing Christ through Scriptures at the Paschal Celebration: Exegesis as Mystery Performance in the Paschal Writings of Melito, Pseudo-Hippolytus and Origen," *Orientalia christiana periodica* 74 (2008): 27–47.

Stewart-Sykes, A. *The Lamb's High Feast: Melito, Peri Pascha and the Quartodeciman Paschal Liturgy at Sardis*. Leiden: Brill, 1998.

Jewish and Christian Paschal liturgies

Bahr, Gordon J. "The Seder of Passover and the Eucharistic Words." *Novum Testamentum* 12 (1970): 181–202.

Bokser, Baruch M. *The Origins of the Seder: The Passover Rite and Early Rabbinic Judaism*. Berkeley: University of California, 1984.

Carmichael, Deborah Bleicher. "David Daube on the Eucharist and the Passover Seder." *Journal for the Study of the New Testament* 42 (1991): 45–67.

Daube, David. *He That Cometh*. London: Diocese of London, 1966.
_____. *Wine in the Bible*. London: Diocese of London, 1974.

Gerlach, Karl. *The Ante-Nicene Pascha: A Rhetorical History*. Leuven: Peeters, 1998.

Giulea, Dragoş-Andrei. *Pre-Nicene Christology in Paschal Contexts: The Case of the Divine Noetic Anthropos*. Leiden: Brill, 2014.

Hall, S. G. "Melito in the Light of the Passover Haggadah." *Journal of Theological Studies* 22 (1971): 29–46.

Jeremias, J. *The Eucharistic Words of Jesus* (ETr). London: SCM, 1966.

Leonhard, Clemens. *The Jewish Pesach and the Origins of Christian Easter*. Berlin: De Gruyter, 2006.

Rouwhorst, G. A. M. "The Quartodeciman Passover and the Jewish Pesach." *Questions Liturgiques* 77 (1996): 152–73

Stein, S. "The Influence of Symposia Literature on the Literary Form of the Pesah Haggadah." *Journal of Jewish Studies* 8 (1957): 13–44

Trocmé, Étienne. *The Passion as Liturgy* (ETr). London: SCM, 1983.

Zeitlin, Solomon. "The Liturgy of the First Night of Passover." *Jewish Quarterly Review* 38 (1947–8): 431–60.

Sardis

Hanfmann, G. M. A., Fikret Yegül, and John S. Crawford. "The Roman and Late Antique Period." In *Sardis from Prehistoric to Roman Times: Results of the Archaeological Exploration of Sardis 1958–1975,* edited by G. M. A. Hanfmann, 139–67 (Cambridge, MA: Harvard UP, 1983).

Hanfmann, G. M. A., and Hans Buchwald. "Christianity: Churches and Cemeteries." In *Sardis from Prehistoric to Roman Times: Results of the Archaeological Exploration of Sardis 1958–1975,* edited by G. M. A. Hanfmann, 191–210 (Cambridge, MA: Harvard UP, 1983).

Mitten, D. G. "A New Look at Ancient Sardis." *Biblical Archaeologist* 29 (1966): 38–68.

Seager, A. R. "The Building History of the Sardis Synagogue." *American Journal of Archaeology* 76 (1972): 425–35.

Trebilco, Paul. *Jewish Communities in Asia Minor.* Cambridge: Cambridge University Press, 1991.

Melito as rhetorician

Manis, A. "Melito of Sardis: Hermeneutic and Context." *Greek Orthodox Theological Review* 32 (1987): 387–401.

Halton, Thomas. "Stylistic Device in Melito, *Peri Pascha.*" In *Kyriakon: Festschrift Johannes Quasten,* edited by Patrick Granfield and Josef A. Jungmann, 249–55. Münster: Aschendorff, 1970.

Wifstrand, A. "The Homily of Melito on the Passion." *Vigiliae Christianae* 2 (1948): 201–23.

Melito and later hymnody and liturgy

Gavrilyuk, Paul. "Melito's Influence upon the Anaphora of *Apostolic Constitutions* 8.12." *Vigiliae Christianae* 59 (2005): 355–76.

Tsakonas, B. G. "The Usage of the Scriptures in the Homily of Melito of Sardis On the Passion." *Theologia* 38 (1967): 609–20.

Wellesz, E. J. "Melito's Homily on the Passion: An Investigation into the Sources of Byzantine Hymnography." *Journal of Theological Studies* 44 (1943): 41–8.

Melito's anti-Judaism

Stewart-Sykes, A. "Melito's Anti-Judaism." *Journal of Early Christian Studies* 5 (1997): 271–83.
Wilson, S. G. "Passover, Easter and Anti-Judaism: Melito of Sardis and Others." In *To See Ourselves as Others See Us: Christians, Jews, "Others" in Late Antiquity,* edited by Jacob Neusner and Ernest S. Frerichs, 337–56. Chico: Scholars, 1985.

Technical historical issues (mentioned but glossed over in the introduction)

Cadman, W. H. "The Christian Pascha and the Day of the Crucifixion: Nisan 14 or 15." *Studia Patristica* 5 (TU 80. Berlin: Akademie, 1962), 8–16.
Dugmore, C. "A Note on the Quartodecimans." *Studia Patristica* 4 (TU 79; Berlin, Akademie, 1961), 411–21.
Hall, S. G. "The Origins of Easter." *Studia Patristica* 15 (TU 128; Berlin, Akademie, 1984), 554–67.
Richardson, Cyril C. "The Quartodecimans and the Synoptic Chronology." *Harvard Theological Review* 33 (1940): 177–90.
———. "A New Solution to the Quartodeciman Riddle." *Journal of Theological Studies* (n.s.) 24 (1973): 74–84. (A recantation of his 1940 work!)

Other literature

Bauckham, Richard. "Papias and Polycrates on the Origin of the Fourth Gospel." *Journal of Theological Studies* (n.s.) 44 (1993): 24–69.
Bradshaw, Paul F., and Maxwell E. Johnson. *The Origins of Feasts, Fasts and Seasons in Early Christianity.* Collegeville, MN: Liturgical Press, 2011.

Bonner, Campbell. *The Homily on the Passion by Melito Bishop of Sardis and Some Fragments of the Apocryphal Ezekiel.* London: Christophers, 1940.

Kahle, P. "Was Melito's Homily on the Passion Originally Written in Syriac?" *Journal of Theological Studies* 44 (1943): 52–6.

Talley, T. J. *The Origins of the Liturgical Year.* Collegeville, MN: Liturgical Press, 1986.

EDITORIAL NOTE ON THE GREEK TEXT

There are two fairly recent critical editions of the Greek text of Melito's *On Pascha*: that of S. G. Hall (*Melito of Sardis: On Pascha and Fragments* [Oxford: Clarendon, 1979]), the basis of the English translation published in this volume, and the earlier edition of Othmar Perler (*Sur la Pâque et fragments de Méliton de Sardes*, Sources chrétiennes, vol. 123 [Paris: Cerf, 1966]), who adopted many readings different from those of Hall. A comparison of the two texts prompted the acceptance of Hall's readings in almost every case. The desire to present a very clean reader's text unencumbered by editorial marks led to the omission of brackets of various sorts, particularly since these would be practically useless without the critical apparatus that accompanied them in the original publication. Nevertheless, Perler's variant readings are noted in a quasi-apparatus; these take the form: line number, the reading in the text (almost always Hall's), colon, Perler's reading. In the few instances where Perler's reading is in the text here offered, Hall's name is mentioned in the apparatus along with his variant. The most common abbreviation in the apparatus is *om.* for "omits" or "omitted." Any reader interested in the niceties and complexities of the text is invited to consult either or both of the critical editions just mentioned.

ΜΕΛΙΤΩΝΟΣ

ΠΕΡΙ ΠΑΣΧΑ

1 Ἡ μὲν γραφὴ τῆς Ἑβραϊκῆς ἐξόδου ἀνέγνωσται
καὶ τὰ ῥήματα τοῦ μυστηρίου διασεσάφηται,
πῶς τὸ πρόβατον θύεται
καὶ πῶς ὁ λαὸς σῴζεται
καὶ πῶς ὁ Φαραὼ διὰ τοῦ μυστηρίου μαστίζεται.   5

2 τοίνυν ξύνετε, ὦ ἀγαπητοί,
ὅπως ἐστὶν καινὸν καὶ παλαιόν,
ἀΐδιον καὶ πρόσκαιρον,
φθαρτὸν καὶ ἄφθαρτον,
θνητὸν καὶ ἀθάνατον τὸ τοῦ πάσχα μυστήριον·   10

3 παλαιὸν μὲν κατὰ τὸν νόμον,
καινὸν δὲ κατὰ τὸν λόγον·

5 The line is Hall's back-translation from the Latin; it is not found in
Perler's text.

On Pascha

1 The Scripture of the exodus of the Hebrews has been read,
and the words of the mystery have been declared;[1]
    how the sheep was sacrificed,
    and how the people was saved,
    and how Pharaoh was flogged by the mystery.

2 Therefore, well-beloved, understand,
    how the mystery of the Pascha
      is both new and old,
      eternal and provisional,
      perishable and imperishable,
      mortal and immortal.

3 It is old with respect to the law,
    new with respect to the word.

---

[1]The meaning of this opening phrase has been much debated. In particular, two assertions have been made which affect its interpretation:

a) That the Scripture was read in Hebrew and

b) That the second line refers to another process intervening between the reading and the delivery of *On Pascha*, for instance a translation of the Hebrew text (on the assumption that the text was read in Hebrew) or else a preliminary treatment (something like the *enarratio*, which was a standard practice of the schools after a reading).

The translation here reflects the belief that neither assertion is true. The Scripture was not read in Hebrew (the exodus is that "of the Hebrews" and not "in Hebrew") and the second line is a couplet lending solemnity to the description of the proceedings. *On Pascha*, or at least part of *On Pascha*, is the *enarratio*, as Melito himself makes clear. For details of the discussion and bibliography see Alistair Stewart-Sykes, *The Lamb's High Feast* (Leiden: Brill, 1998), 96–9, 172–6.

πρόσκαιρον κατὰ τὸν τύπον,
ἀΐδιον διὰ τὴν χάριν·
φθαρτὸν διὰ τὴν τοῦ προβάτου σφαγήν,   15
ἄφθαρτον διὰ τὴν τοῦ κυρίου ζωήν·
θνητὸν διὰ τὴν εἰς γῆν ταφήν,
ἀθάνατον διὰ τὴν ἐκ νεκρῶν ἀνάστασιν.

4   παλαιὸς μὲν ὁ νόμος,
    καινὸς δὲ ὁ λόγος·   20
    πρόσκαιρος ὁ τύπος,
    ἀΐδιος δὲ ἡ χάρις·
    φθαρτὸν τὸ πρόβατον,
    ἄφθαρτος ὁ κύριος·
    μὴ συντριβεὶς ὡς ἀμνός,   25
    ἀνασταθεὶς δὲ ὡς θεός.
    εἰ καὶ γὰρ ὡς πρόβατον εἰς σφαγὴν ἤχθη,
    ἀλλ᾽ οὐκ ἦν πρόβατον·
    εἰ καὶ ὡς ἀμνὸς ἄφωνος,
    ἀλλ᾽ οὐδὲ ἀμνὸς ἦν.   30
    ὁ μὲν γὰρ τύπος ἐγένετο,
    ἡ δὲ ἀλήθεια ηὑρίσκετο.

5   ἀντὶ γὰρ τοῦ ἀμνοῦ υἱὸς ἐγένετο
    καὶ ἀντὶ τοῦ προβάτου ἄνθρωπος,
    ἐν δὲ τῷ ἀνθρώπῳ Χριστὸς ὃς κεχώρηκεν τὰ πάντα.   35

6   ἡ γοῦν τοῦ προβάτου σφαγὴ
    καὶ ἡ τοῦ αἵματος πομπὴ

13 κατὰ: διὰ   17 εἰς γῆν: ἐν τῇ γῇ
25 μὴ συντριβεὶς: σφαγεὶς   26 ἀνασταθεὶς: ἀναστὰς
27 εἰ: om.   28 οὐκ ἦν πρόβατον: οὐδὲ πρόβατον ἦν
29 εἰ: om.   33 υἱὸς: θεὸς
37 αἵματος: πάσχα

Provisional with respect to the type,[2]
   yet everlasting through grace.
It is perishable because of the slaughter of the sheep,
   imperishable because of the life of the Lord.
It is mortal because of the burial in the ground,
   immortal because of the resurrection from the dead.

4   For the law is old,
   but the word is new.
The type is provisional,
   but grace is everlasting.
The sheep is perishable,
   but the Lord,
not broken as a lamb but raised up as God,
   is imperishable.
For though led to the slaughter like a sheep
   he was no sheep.
Though speechless as a lamb,
   neither yet was he a lamb.
For there was once a type, but now the reality has appeared.

5   For instead of the lamb there was a son,
   and instead of the sheep a man;
in the man was Christ encompassing all things.

6   So the slaughter of the sheep,
   and the sacrificial procession of the blood,[3]

[2] The word here rendered "type" is intended by Melito to indicate that the events of the old covenant are models of what would occur under the new covenant. He explains his theory of typology below at sections 34–45. The word is used by many patristic writers, but precise understandings of the relationship between the type and the reality, or fulfillment, vary. In essence the idea of typology is that the events of the old covenant were intended to lead to the greater perfection of the new covenant. See further the introduction pp. 42–44.

[3] The word translated here as "sacrificial procession" (*pompē*) generally means simply procession. Pindar (*Ode* 7.80) however uses it to refer to a sacrificial procession with a sheep, and it is far from impossible that Melito is alluding to this usage.

καὶ ἡ τοῦ νόμου γραφὴ εἰς Χριστὸν Ἰησοῦν κεχώρηκεν,
δι᾽ ὃν τὰ πάντα ἐν τῷ πρεσβυτέρῳ νόμῳ ἐγένετο,
μᾶλλον δὲ ἐν τῷ νέῳ λόγῳ. 40

7 καὶ γὰρ ὁ νόμος λόγος ἐγένετο,
 καὶ ὁ παλαιὸς καινός,
  συνεξελθὼν ἐκ Σιὼν καὶ Ἰερουσαλήμ,
 καὶ ἡ ἐντολὴ χάρις,
 καὶ ὁ τύπος ἀλήθεια, 45
 καὶ ὁ ἀμνὸς υἱός,
 καὶ τὸ πρόβατον ἄνθρωπος,
 καὶ ὁ ἄνθρωπος θεός.

8 ὡς γὰρ υἱὸς τεχθείς,
 καὶ ὡς ἀμνὸς ἀχθείς, 50
 καὶ ὡς πρόβατον σφαγείς,
 καὶ ὡς ἄνθρωπος ταφείς,
 ἀνέστη ἐκ νεκρῶν ὡς θεὸς φύσει θεὸς ὢν καὶ ἄνθρωπος.

9 ὅς ἐστιν τὰ πάντα·
 καθ᾽ ὃ κρίνει νόμος, 55
 καθ᾽ ὃ διδάσκει λόγος,
 καθ᾽ ὃ σῴζει χάρις,
 καθ᾽ ὃ γεννᾷ πατήρ,
 καθ᾽ ὃ γεννᾶται υἱός,
 καθ᾽ ὃ πάσχει πρόβατον, 60

and the writing of the law encompass Christ,
on whose account everything in the previous law took place,
   though better in the new dispensation.

7 For the law was a word,
    and the old was new,
      going out from Sion and Jerusalem,
    and the commandment was grace,
    and the type was a reality,
    and the lamb was a son,
    and the sheep was a man,
    and the man was God.

8 For he was born a son,
    and led as a lamb,
    and slaughtered as a sheep,
    and buried as a man,
    and rose from the dead as God,
  being God by his nature and a man.

9 He is all things.
    He is law, in that he judges.
    He is word, in that he teaches.
    He is grace, in that he saves.
    He is father, in that he begets.[4]
    He is son, in that he is begotten.
    He is sheep, in that he suffers.

---

[4]Note that Christ himself is described here as father! This is an example of the christocentric monotheism, espoused by Melito. In time such a view of Christ became recognized as heretical because of its inadequacies, and in more recent times Melito has been labelled on this basis a "naive modalist." However, the complexities of Trinitarian relationships had not been discussed in the time of Melito and so Melito simply espouses what is essentially a traditional Asian understanding, also found in the work of Ignatius of Antioch. For further discussion of Melito's Christology see the introduction above pp. 39–40.

καθ' ὃ θάπτεται ἄνθρωπος,
καθ' ὃ ἀνίσταται θεός.

10 οὗτός ἐστιν Ἰησοῦς ὁ Χριστός,
ᾧ ἡ δόξα εἰς τοὺς αἰῶνας τῶν αἰώνων. ἀμήν.

11 Τοῦτό ἐστιν τὸ τοῦ πάσχα μυστήριον   65
καθὼς ἐν τῷ νόμῳ γέγραπται,
ὡς μικρῷ πρόσθεν ἀνέγνωσται·
διηγήσομαι δὲ τὰ ῥήματα τῆς γραφῆς,
πῶς ὁ θεὸς ἐντέταλται Μωυσεῖ ἐν Αἰγύπτῳ,
ὁπότε βούλεται τὸν μὲν Φαραὼ δῆσαι ὑπὸ μάστιγα,   70
τὸν δὲ Ἰσραὴλ λῦσαι ἀπὸ μάστιγος διὰ χειρὸς Μωυσέως.

12 Ἰδοὺ γάρ, φησίν, λήμψῃ ἄσπιλον ἀμνὸν καὶ ἄμωμον,
καὶ προς ἑσπέραν σφάξεις αὐτὸν μετὰ τῶν υἱῶν Ἰσραήλ,
καὶ νύκτωρ ἔδεσθε αὐτὸ μετὰ σπουδῆς·
ὀστοῦν οὐ συντρίψεις αὐτοῦ.   75

13 οὕτως, φησίν, ποιήσεις.
ἐν μιᾷ νυκτὶ ἔδεσθε αὐτὸ κατὰ πατριὰς καὶ δήμους,
περιεζωσμένοι τὰς ὀσφύας ὑμῶν
καὶ αἱ ῥάβδοι ἐν ταῖς χερσὶν ὑμῶν.

70 ὁπότε: ὁπόταν
73 πρὸς ἑσπέραν: ἑσπέρας
74 αὐτὸ: αὐτὸν
75 ὀστοῦν: καὶ ὀστοῦν   συντρίψεις: συντρίψετε
77 αὐτὸ: αὐτὸν

He is human, in that he is buried.
He is God, in that he is raised up.

10 This is Jesus the Christ,
to whom be the glory for ever and ever. Amen.[5]

11 This is the mystery of the Pascha,
just as it is written in the law, which was read a little while
ago.
I shall narrate the scriptural story,[6]
how he gave command to Moses in Egypt
when wanting to flog Pharaoh
and to free Israel from flogging
through the hand of Moses.

12 "Look," he says, "you shall take a lamb, without spot or
blemish,
and, toward the evening, slaughter it with the sons of Israel.
And eat it at night with haste.
And not a bone of it shall you break."

13 "This is what you shall do," he says:
"You shall eat it in one night by families and tribes
with your loins girded up
and with staves in your hands.

[5]This doxology divides off the first portion of the work. As was observed in the introduction, in Graeco-Roman rhetoric it was usual to start by setting out what the speech would achieve in a section known as the *thesis* or *propositio*. In this opening Melito sets out the fundamental theme of *On Pascha*, namely the substitution of the Christian Pascha for the Jewish Pesah through the resurrection triumph of Jesus.

[6]By stating that he will tell the story from Scripture, Melito is informing his audience that the part of his speech which is now beginning is the *diēgēma*, or *narratio*, the narrative which lays down the basis for the remainder of the speech (the confirmation or denial). Beyond this however we must note that in Scripture the telling of the works of God is a significant part of praise. Melito unites the scriptural tradition with that of classical rhetoric by giving praise whilst laying down the *narratio* of his declamation.

ἔστιν γὰρ τοῦτο πάσχα κυρίου,   80
μνημόσυνον αἰώνιον τοῖς υἱοῖς Ἰσραήλ.

14 λαβόντες δὲ τὸ τοῦ προβάτου αἷμα
χρίσατε τὰ πρόθυρα τῶν οἰκιῶν ὑμῶν,
τιθέντες ἐπὶ τοὺς σταθμοὺς τῆς εἰσόδου
τὸ σημεῖον τοῦ αἵματος εἰς δυσωπίαν τοῦ ἀγγέλου.   85
ἰδοὺ γὰρ, πατάσσω Αἴγυπτον
καὶ ἐν μιᾷ νυκτὶ ἀτεκνωθήσεται ἀπὸ κτήνους ἕως
ἀνθρώπου.

15 τότε Μωυσῆς σφάξας τὸ πρόβατον
καὶ νύκτωρ διατελέσας τὸ μυστήριον μετὰ τῶν υἱῶν
Ἰσραὴλ
ἐσφράγισεν τὰς τῶν οἰκιῶν θύρας   90
εἰς φρουρὰν τοῦ λαοῦ καὶ εἰς δυσωπίαν τοῦ ἀγγέλου.

16 Ὁπότε δὲ τὸ πρόβατον σφάζεται
καὶ τὸ πάσχα βιβρώσκεται
καὶ τὸ μυστήριον τελεῖται
καὶ ὁ λαὸς εὐφραίνεται   95
καὶ ὁ Ἰσραὴλ σφραγίζεται,
τότε ἀφίκετο ὁ ἄγγελος πατάσσειν Αἴγυπτον,
τὴν ἀμύητον τοῦ μυστηρίου,

86 πατάσσω: πατάξω

This is the Passover of the Lord,
a commemoration to the sons of Israel for ever."

14 "Taking the blood of the sheep
you shall anoint the front doors of your houses
putting blood on the doorposts of the entrances;
the sign of the blood to avert the angel.
For behold, I shall strike Egypt
and in one night shall both beast and man be made
childless."

15 Then Moses, having slaughtered the sheep
and performed the mystery at night with the sons of Israel,[7]
sealed the doors of the houses to protect the people
and to avert the angel.[8]

16 But while the sheep is being slaughtered,
and the Pascha is being eaten,
and the mystery is completed,
and the people is rejoicing,
and Israel is being sealed:
then came the angel to strike Egypt,
those uninitiated in the mystery,

[7] Although this language is obviously redolent of the mystery religions, more influential is Melito's own experience of a nocturnal commemoration.

[8] This passage is full of allusions to Exodus 12 but is very much a free retelling, far freer than the targums, or Jewish translations of the Scriptures, which were in contemporary use. The instruction not to break a bone of the animal was clearly significant in the light of the Johannine association of Jesus and the Passover lamb since John quotes the same text in referring to the death of Jesus at the time the lambs were being slaughtered in the Temple (Jn 19.36). Although Melito renders Exodus very freely here, this instruction is found in the Septuagint in a very different place from that of the Hebrew text. Therefore, Melito here would seem either to be using a Hebrew text or another Greek translation, but not the Septuagint. In describing the Pascha as an apotropaic rite, Melito insinuates much language relating to Christian initiation. One should not however conclude from this language that initiation was necessarily practiced at Pascha in Melito's time.

τὴν ἄμοιρον τοῦ πάσχα,
τὴν ἀσφράγιστον τοῦ αἵματος,   100
τὴν ἀφρούρητον τοῦ πνεύματος,
τὴν ἔχθραν,
τὴν ἄπιστον·
ἐν μιᾷ νυκτὶ πατάξας ἠτέκνωσεν.

17 περιελθὼν γὰρ τὸν Ἰσραὴλ ὁ ἄγγελος   105
     καὶ ἰδὼν ἐσφραγισμένον τῷ τοῦ προβάτου αἵματι,
     ἦλθεν ἐπ᾽ Αἴγυπτον,
     καὶ τὸν σκληροτράχηλον Φαραὼ διὰ πένθους ἐδάμασεν,
     ἐνδύσας αὐτὸν οὐ στόλην φαιὰν
     οὐδὲ πέπλον περιεσχισμένον,   110
     ἀλλ᾽ ὅλην Αἴγυπτον περιεσχισμένην,
     πενθοῦσαν ἐπὶ τοῖς πρωτοτόκοις αὐτῆς.

18 ὅλη γὰρ Αἴγυπτος γενηθεῖσα ἐν πόνοις καὶ πληγαῖς,
     ἐν δάκρυσιν καὶ κοπετοῖς,
     ἀφίκετο πρὸς Φαραὼ ὅλη πενθήρης,   115
     οὐ μόνον τῷ σχήματι ἀλλὰ καὶ τῇ ψυχῇ,
     περιεσχισμένη οὐ μόνον τὰς στολὰς τῆς περιβολῆς
     ἀλλὰ καὶ τοὺς μασθοὺς τῆς τρυφῆς.

19 ἦν δὲ καινὸν θέαμα ἰδεῖν,
     ἔνθα κοπτομένους ἔνθα κωκύοντας,   120
     καὶ μέσον Φαραὼ πενθήρη
          ἐπὶ σάκκῳ καὶ σπόδῳ καθήμενον,
     περιβεβλημένον τὸ ψηλαφητὸν σκότος ὡς ἱμάτιον
          πενθικόν,
     περιεζωσμένον ὅλην Αἴγυπτον ὡς κιθῶνα πένθους.

118 μασθοὺς: μαστοὺς

those with no part in the Pascha,
those not sealed by the blood,
those not guarded by the Spirit,
the hostile,
the faithless;
in one night he struck them and made them childless.

17 For the angel had passed by Israel,
and seen him sealed with the blood of the sheep,
he fell upon Egypt,
he tamed stiff-necked Pharaoh with grief,
clothing him not with a garment of grey,
nor with a tunic all torn,
but with all Egypt torn and grieving for her first-born.

18 For all Egypt was pained and grieving,
in tears and mourning,
and came to Pharaoh stricken with woe
not outwardly only but inwardly.
Not only were her garments torn
but also her delicate breasts.

19 It was indeed a strange spectacle,
here people beating their breasts, there people wailing,
and grief-stricken Pharaoh in the middle,
seated on sackcloth and ashes,
palpable darkness thrown around him as a mourning
cloak,
clad in all Egypt like a tunic of grief.[9]

---

[9]The theatrical imagery employed here is common in the rhetoric of the second century. Pharaoh is depicted as a tragic figure, surrounded by the chorus, the people of Egypt.

20 ἦν γὰρ περικειμένη Αἴγυπτος τὸν Φαραὼ   125
        ὡς περιβολὴ κωκυτοῦ.
    τοιοῦτος ὑφάνθη κιθὼν τῷ τυραννικῷ σώματι,
    τοιαύτην ἐνέδυσεν στολὴν τὸν σκληρὸν Φαραὼ
        ὁ τῆς δικαιοσύνης ἄγγελος·
        πένθος πικρὸν καὶ σκότος ψηλαφητόν,   130
        καὶ ἀτεκνίαν καινὴν ἐπὶ τῶν πρωτοτόκων αὐτῆς.

21 ἦν γὰρ ταχινὸς καὶ ἀκόρεστος ὁ τῶν πρωτοτόκων θάνατος,
    ἦν [δὲ] καινὸν τρόπαιον ἰδεῖν
        ἐπὶ τῶν πιπτόντων νεκρῶν ἐν μιᾷ ῥοπῇ.
    καὶ ἐγένετο τοῦ θανάτου τροφὴ   135
        ἡ τῶν κειμένων τροπή.

22 καινὴν δὲ συμφορὰν ἐὰν ἀκούσητε θαυμάσετε·
    τάδε γὰρ περιέσχεν τοὺς Αἰγυπτίους,
        νὺξ μακρὰ
        καὶ σκότος ψηλαφητὸν   140
        καὶ θάνατος ψηλαφῶν
        καὶ ἄγγελος ἐκθλίβων
        καὶ ᾅδης καταπίνων τοὺς πρωτοτόκους αὐτῶν.

23 τὸ δὲ καινότερον καὶ φοβερώτερον ἀκοῦσαι ἔχετε·
    ἐν τῷ ψηλαφητῷ σκότει ὁ ἀψηλάφητος θάνατος ἐκρύβετο,145
        καὶ τὸ μὲν σκότος ἐψηλάφων οἱ δυστυχεῖς Αἰγύπτιοι,
        ὁ δὲ θάνατος ἐξεραυνῶν ἐψηλάφα τοὺς πρωτοτόκους τῶν
            Αἰγυπτίων
        τοῦ ἀγγέλου κελεύοντος.

131 καινὴν: καὶ ἦν

20 For Egypt was surrounding Pharaoh
        like a robe of wailing.
    Such a tunic was woven for the tyrannical body,
    With such a garment did the angel of justice
        clothe unyielding Pharaoh:
      bitter grief and palpable darkness
      and a strange childlessness, the loss of her first-born.

21 The death of the first-born was swift and greedy,
        it was a strange trophy on which to gaze,
    upon those falling dead in one moment.
        And the food of death was the defeat of the prostrate.

22 Listen and wonder at a new disaster,
      for these things enclosed the Egyptians:
        long night,
        palpable darkness,
        death grasping,
        the angel squeezing out the life,
        and Hades gulping down the first-born.[10]

23 But the strangest and most terrifying thing you are yet to
    hear:
    In the palpable darkness hid untouchable death,
        and the wretched Egyptians were grasping the darkness,
        while death sought out and grasped the Egyptian first-born
            at the angel's command.[11]

---

[10]The description of death grasping the firstborn is reminiscent of Homer's description of blinded cyclops grasping for his victims, according to Thomas Halton, "Stylistic Device in Melito, *Peri Pascha*," in *Kyriakon: Festschrift Johannes Quasten,* ed. Patrick Granfield and Josef A. Jungmann (Münster: Aschendorff, 1970), 249–55. In Melito's use of the word *katapinō* to describe the manner in which Hades swallows the first-born we may perhaps also discern echoes of Hesiod's description of Kronos swallowing his offspring.

[11]On this passage Karl Gerlach, *The Ante-Nicene Pascha: A Rhetorical History* (Leuven: Peeters, 1998), 64–65, comments: "The 'grasping darkness' is not just

24 εἴ τις οὖν ἐψηλάφα τὸ σκότος
      ὑπὸ τοῦ θανάτου ἐξήγετο.   150
    καί τις πρωτότοκος χειρὶ σκοτεινὸν σῶμα ἐναγκαλισάμενος,
      τῇ ψυχῇ ἐκδειματωθεὶς οἰκτρὸν καὶ φοβερὸν ἀνεβόησεν·
    Τίνα κρατεῖ ἡ δεξιά μου;
      τίνα τρέμει ἡ ψυχή μου;
      τίς μοι σκοτεινὸς περικέχυται ὅλῳ τῷ σώματι;   155
      εἰ μὲν πατήρ, βοήθησον·
      εἰ δὲ μήτηρ, συμπάθησον·
      εἰ δὲ ἀδελφός, προσλάλησον·
      εἰ δὲ φίλος, συστάθητι·
      εἰ δὲ ἐχθρός, ἀπαλλάγηθι, ὅτι πρωτότοκος ἐγώ.   160

25 πρὸ δὲ τοῦ σιωπῆσαι τὸν πρωτότοκον
      ἡ μακρὰ σιωπὴ κατέσχεν αὐτὸν προσειποῦσα·
    Πρωτότοκος ἐμὸς εἶ·
    ἐγώ σοι πέπρωμαι ἡ τοῦ θανάτου σιωπή.

26 ἕτερος δέ τις πρωτότοκος νοήσας τὴν τῶν πρωτοτόκων
      ἅλωσιν   165
      ἑαυτὸν ἀπαρνεῖτο ἵνα μὴ θάνῃ πικρῶς·
    Οὔκ εἰμι πρωτότοκος,
    τριτῷ γεγέννημαι καρπῷ.
    ὁ δὲ ψευσθῆναι μὴ δυνάμενος τοῦ πρωτοτόκου προσήπτετο,
      πρηνὴς δὲ ἔπιπτεν σιγῶν.   170

150 ὑπὸ: ὑπὲρ
151 καί: εἴ
159 συστάθητι: εὐστάθησον

24 If anyone grasped the darkness
        he was pulled away by death.
    And one of the first-born,
        grasping the material darkness in his hand,
        as his life was stripped away,
        cried out in distress and terror:
        "Whom does my hand hold?
        Whom does my soul dread?
        Who is the dark one enfolding my whole body?
        If it is a father, help me.
        If it is a mother, comfort me.
        If it is a brother, speak to me.
        If it is a friend, support me.
        If it is an enemy, depart from me, for I am a first-born."

25 Before the first-born fell silent, the long silence held him and
    spoke to him:
        You are my first-born,
        I am your destiny, the silence of death.[12]

26 Another first-born, perceiving the seizure of the first-born,
        denied himself, so not bitterly to die:
        "I am not a first-born,
        I was begotten third."
    But the one who could not be deceived fastened on the first-
        born
        who fell silently down.

---

melodrama, but embraces the delivery of the homily in a dark place where Christians have gathered on the paschal night with only a few candles or torches for light. Rhetorically, Melito's hearers are being killed off one by one, except for the sign of blood."

[12]Here is another classical reference, this time to Aeschylus, *Eumenides* 935; it is not coincidental that the allusion is from a theatrical piece, since the manner in which Melito self-consciously stands as reporter is rather like that of a messenger-speech in Greek tragedy.

ὑπὸ δὲ μίαν ῥοπὴν ὁ πρωτότοκος καρπὸς τῶν Αἰγυπτίων
    ἀπώλετο·
ὁ πρωτόσπορος,
ὁ πρωτότοκος,
ὁ ποθητός,
ὁ περίψυκτος ἠδαφίσθη χαμαί·   175
οὐχ ὁ τῶν ἀνθρώπων μόνον,
    ἀλλὰ καὶ τῶν ἀλόγων ζώων.

27 μύκημα δὲ ἐν τοῖς πεδίοις τῆς γῆς ἠκούετο
    ἀποδυρομένων κτηνῶν ἐπὶ τῶν τροφίμων αὐτῶν·
    καὶ γὰρ δάμαλις ὑπόμοσχος   180
    καὶ ἵππος ὑπόπωλος
    καὶ τὰ λοιπὰ κτήνη λοχευόμενα καὶ σπαργῶντα
    πικρὸν καὶ ἐλεεινὸν ἀπωδύροντο ἐπὶ τῶν πρωτοτόκων
        καρπῶν.

28 οἰμωγὴ δέ τις καὶ κοπετὸς ἐπὶ τῇ τῶν ἀνθρώπων ἀπωλείᾳ
    ἐγένετο,
        ἐπὶ τῇ τῶν πρωτοτόκων νεκρῶν.   185
    ὅλη γὰρ ἐπώζεσεν Αἴγυπτος ἐπὶ τῶν ἀτάφων σωμάτων.

29 ἦν δὲ θεάσασθαι φοβερὸν θέαμα
    τῶν Αἰγυπτίων μητέρας λυσικόμους,
        πατέρας λυσίφρονας,
    δεινὸν ἀνακωκύοντας τῇ Αἰγυπτιακῇ φωνῇ·   190
    Δυστυχεῖς ἠτεκνώμεθα ὑπὸ μίαν ῥοπὴν ἀπὸ τοῦ
        πρωτοτόκου καρποῦ.
    ἦσαν δὲ ἐπὶ μαστῶν κοπτόμενοι,
        χερσὶν τύπτοντες κροτήματα ἐπὶ τῆς τῶν νεκρῶν
            ὀρχήσεως.

184 τις: om.
192 μασθῶν: μαστῶν

At one moment the first-born fruit of the Egyptians was
    destroyed,
  the first-begotten, the first-born,
  not human only but of dumb beasts,
  the desired,
    the fondled one, was dashed downward.

27 A lowing was heard in the plains of the land,
    the moaning of beasts over their sucklings,
  the cow with sucking calf and the horse with foal,
    and the rest of the beasts bearing young and carrying milk,
    and their moaning over their first-born
  was bitter and piteous.

28 At the human loss there was howling and grief
    over the dead first-born,
  and all Egypt was stinking with unburied bodies.

29 It was a terrible spectacle to watch,
    the mothers of the Egyptians with hair undone,
      the fathers with minds undone,
    wailing terribly in the Egyptian tongue:
      "By evil chance we are bereaved in a moment of our first-
      born issue."
    They were beating their breasts,
      they were tapping time with their hands for the dance of
      the dead.

30 Τοιαύτη συμφορὰ περιέσχεν Αἴγυπτον,
       ἄφνω δὲ ἠτέκνωσεν αὐτήν.   195
       ἦν δὲ ὁ Ἰσραὴλ φρουρούμενος ὑπὸ τῆς τοῦ προβάτου σφαγῆς,
       καί γε συνεφωτίζετο ὑπὸ τοῦ χυθέντος αἵματος,
       καὶ τεῖχος ηὑρίσκετο τοῦ λαοῦ ὁ τοῦ προβάτου θάνατος.

31 ὢ μυστηρίου καινοῦ καὶ ἀνεκδιηγήτου·
       ἡ τοῦ προβάτου σφαγὴ ηὑρίσκετο τοῦ Ἰσραὴλ σωτηρία,   200
       καὶ ὁ τοῦ προβάτου θάνατος ζωὴ τοῦ λαοῦ ἐγένετο,
       καὶ τὸ αἷμα ἐδυσώπησεν τὸν ἄγγελον.

32 λέγε μοι, ὢ ἄγγελε, τί ἐδυσωπήθης;
       τὴν τοῦ προβάτου σφαγὴν ἢ τὴν τοῦ κυρίου ζωήν;
       τὸν τοῦ προβάτου θάνατον ἢ τὸν τοῦ κυρίου τύπον;   205
       τὸ τοῦ προβάτου αἷμα ἢ τὸ τοῦ κυρίου πνεῦμα;

33 δῆλος εἶ δυσωπηθεὶς
       ἰδὼν τὸ τοῦ κυρίου μυστήριον ἐν τῷ προβάτῳ γινόμενον,
       τὴν τοῦ κυρίου ζωὴν ἐν τῇ τοῦ προβάτου σφαγῇ,
       τὸν τοῦ κυρίου τύπον ἐν τῷ τοῦ προβάτου θανάτῳ,   210
       διὰ τοῦτο οὐκ ἐπάταξας τὸν Ἰσραὴλ
       ἀλλὰ μόνην Αἴγυπτον ἠτέκνωσας.

34 Τί τοῦτο τὸ καινὸν μυστήριον,
       Αἴγυπτον μὲν παταχθῆναι εἰς ἀπώλειαν,
       τὸν δὲ Ἰσραὴλ φυλαχθῆναι εἰς σωτηρίαν;   215
       ἀκούσατε τὴν δύναμιν τοῦ μυστηρίου.

30 Such was the calamity which surrounded Egypt,
    and made her suddenly childless.
  Israel was guarded by the slaughter of the sheep,
    and was illuminated by the shedding of blood,
  and the death of the sheep was a wall for the people.

31 O strange and ineffable mystery!
    The slaughter of the sheep was Israel's salvation,
    and the death of the sheep was life for the people,
      and the blood averted the angel.

32 Tell me angel, what turned you away?[13]
    The slaughter of the sheep or the life of the Lord?
    The death of the sheep or the type of the Lord?
    The blood of the sheep or the Spirit of the Lord?

33 It is clear that you turned away
    seeing the mystery of the Lord in the sheep
      and the life of the Lord in the slaughter of the sheep
      and the type of the Lord in the death of the sheep.
    Therefore, you struck not Israel down,
      but made Egypt alone childless.

34 What is this strange mystery,
    that Egypt is struck down for destruction
    and Israel is guarded for salvation?
  Listen to the meaning of the mystery.[14]

---

[13]The sudden address to the angel is again typical of rhetorical practice at the time of Melito.

[14]The word translated here as "meaning," *dynamis*, is employed by rhetorical writers to mean the persuasive effect of oratory, (Lucian, *How to Write History* 34) or of individual units of a speech such as the choice of sounds (so Quintilian, *Beginning Public Speaking* 2.15.3–4, with reference to Ps.-Isocrates; Dionysius of Halicarnassus, *On Composition* 12) The source of this usage is probably Plato, who discusses the *dynamis* of words with reference to their construction (*Cratylus* 394B). What follows does not fit into the rhetorical plan of *On Pascha* but casts light nonetheless on what

35 οὐδέν ἐστιν, ἀγαπητοί, τὸ λεγόμενον καὶ γινόμενον
        δίχα παραβολῆς καὶ προκεντήματος.
    πάντα ὅσα ἐὰν γίνηται καὶ λέγηται παραβολῆς τυγχάνει,
        τὸ μὲν λεγόμενον παραβολῆς,   220
        τὸ δὲ γινόμενον προτυπώσεως·
    ἵνα ὡς ἂν τὸ γινόμενον διὰ τῆς προτυπώσεως δείκνυται,
    οὕτως καὶ τὸ λαλούμενον διὰ τῆς παραβολῆς φωτισθῇ.

36 τοῦτο δὴ γίνεται ἐπὶ προκατασκευῆς·
        ἔργον οὐκ ἀνίσταται,   225
    διὰ δὲ τὸ μέλλον διὰ τῆς τυπικῆς εἰκόνος ὁρᾶσθαι·
    διὰ τοῦτο τοῦ μέλλοντος γίνεται προκέντημα
        ἢ ἐκ κηροῦ ἢ ἐκ πηλοῦ ἢ ἐκ ξύλου,
    ἵνα τὸ μέλλον ἀνίστασθαι
        ὑψηλότερον ἐν μεγέθει   230
        καὶ ἰσχυρότερον ἐν δυνάμει
        καὶ καλὸν ἐν σχήματι
        καὶ πλούσιον ἐν τῇ κατασκευῇ
    διὰ μικροῦ καὶ φθαρτοῦ προκεντήματος ὁραθῇ.

37 ὁπόταν δὲ ἀναστῇ πρὸς ὃ ὁ τύπος,   235
    τό ποτε τοῦ μέλλοντος τὴν εἰκόνα φέρον,
        τοῦτ᾽ ὡς ἄχρηστον γινόμενον λύεται,
    παραχωρῆσαν τῷ φύσει ἀληθεῖ τὴν περὶ αὐτοῦ εἰκόνα.
    γίνεται δὲ τό ποτε τίμιον ἄτιμον
        τοῦ φύσει τιμίου φανερωθέντος.   240

38 ἑκάστῳ γὰρ ἴδιος καιρός·
        ἴδιος χρόνος τοῦ τύπου,
        ἴδιος χρόνος τῆς ὕλης,
        ἴδιος χρόνος τῆς ἀληθείας.

219 γίνηται: γίνεται   λέγηται: λέγεται
223 λαλούμενον: λεγόμενον   224 τοῦτο δὴ γίνεται: εἰ μὴ
226 διὰ δὲ: ἢ οὖ   ὁρᾶσθαι: ὁρᾶται   227 τοῦτο: τοῦτο δὴ
242 ἴδιος χρόνος τοῦ τύπου: τοῦ τύπου ἴδιος χρόνος

35 Nothing, beloved, is spoken or made without an analogy and
a sketch;
for everything which is made and spoken has its analogy,
what is spoken an analogy, what is made a prototype,
so that whatever is made may be perceived through the
prototype
and whatever is spoken clarified by the illustration.

36 This is what occurs in the case of a first draft;
it is not a finished work but exists so that, through the
model, that which is to be can be seen.
Therefore, a preliminary sketch is made of what is to be,
from wax or from clay or from wood,
so that what will come about,
taller in height,
and greater in strength,
and more attractive in shape,
and wealthier in workmanship,
can be seen through the small and provisional sketch.

37 When the thing comes about of which the sketch was a type,
that which was to be, of which the type bore the likeness,
then the type is destroyed, it has become useless,
it yields up the image to what is truly real.
What was once valuable becomes worthless
when what is of true value appears.

38 To each then is its own time:
the type has its own time,
the material has its own time,
the reality has its own time.

has preceded and what follows. Such a digression was common in the rhetoric of
Melito's period; it was meant to sustain the interest of the audience and, whilst being
a digression, nonetheless to relate to the main content of the speech. This is true of
Melito's digression here.

ποιεῖς τὸν τύπον·   245
τοῦτον ποθεῖς
ὅτι τοῦ μέλλοντος ἐν αὐτῷ τὴν εἰκόνα βλέπεις.
προκομίζεις τὴν ὕλην τῷ τύπῳ·
ταύτην ποθεῖς
διὰ τὸ μέλλον ἐν αὐτῇ ἀνίστασθαι.   250
ἀπαρτίζεις τὸ ἔργον·
τοῦτο μόνον ποθεῖς,
τοῦτο μόνον φιλεῖς,
ἐν αὐτῷ μόνῳ τὸν τύπον καὶ τὴν ὕλην καὶ τὴν ἀλήθειαν βλέπων.

39 Ὡς γοῦν ἐν τοῖς φθαρτοῖς παραδείγμασιν,   255
οὕτως δὴ καὶ ἐν τοῖς ἀφθάρτοις·
ὡς ἐν τοῖς ἐπιγείοις,
οὕτω δὴ καὶ ἐν τοῖς ἐπουρανίοις.
καὶ γὰρ ἡ τοῦ κυρίου σωτηρία καὶ ἀλήθεια ἐν τῷ λαῷ
    προετυπώθη,
καὶ τὰ τοῦ εὐαγγελίου δόγματα ὑπὸ τοῦ νόμου προεκηρύχθη.   260

40 ἐγένετο οὖν ὁ λαὸς τύπος προκεντήματος
    καὶ ὁ νόμος γραφὴ παραβολῆς·
    τὸ δὲ εὐαγγέλιον διήγημα νόμου καὶ πλήρωμα,
    ἡ δὲ ἐκκλησία ἀποδοχεῖον τῆς ἀληθείας.

41 ἦν οὖν ὁ τύπος τίμιος πρὸ τῆς ἀληθείας   265
    καὶ ἦν ἡ παραβολὴ θαυμαστὴ πρὸ τῆς ἑρμενείας·
    τοῦτ' ἔστιν ὁ λαὸς ἦν τίμιος πρὸ τοῦ τὴν ἐκκλησίαν
        ἀνασταθῆναι,
    καὶ ὁ νόμος θαυμαστὸς πρὸ τοῦ τὸ εὐαγγέλιον
        φωτισθῆναι.

243 ἴδιος χρόνος τῆς ὕλης: τῆς ὕλης ἴδιος χρόνος
244 ἴδιος χρόνος: om.
246 τοῦτον: ταύτην Hall
247 αὐτῷ: αὐτῇ Hall   266 ἦν: om.

When you construct the model you require it
  because in it you can see the image of what is to be.
You prepare the material before the model,
  you require it because of what will come about from it.
You complete the work, and that alone you require,
  that alone you desire,
because only there can you see the type, and the material, and
    the reality.

39 So then, just as with the provisional examples
    so it is with eternal things;
  as it is with things on earth
    so it is with the things in heaven.
  For indeed the Lord's salvation and his truth were prefigured
      in the people
  and the decrees of the gospel were proclaimed in advance by
      the law.

40 Thus the people was a type, like a preliminary sketch,
    and the law was the writing of an analogy.
  The gospel is the narrative and fulfillment of the law
    and the Church is the repository of reality.

41 So the type was valuable in advance of the reality
    and the illustration was wonderful before its elucidation.
  So the people were valuable before the Church arose,
    and the law was wonderful before the illumination of the
      gospel.

42 ὁπότε δὲ ἡ ἐκκλησία ἀνέστη
    καὶ τὸ εὐαγγέλιον προέστη,   270
ὁ τύπος ἐκενώθη παραδοὺς τῇ ἀληθείᾳ τὴν δύναμιν,
    καὶ ὁ νόμος ἐπληρώθη παραδοὺς τῷ εὐαγγελίῳ τὴν δύναμιν.

43 ὃν τρόπον ὁ τύπος κενοῦται τῷ φύσει ἀληθεῖ τὴν εἰκόνα
παραδούς,
    καὶ ἡ παραβολὴ πληροῦται ὑπὸ τῆς ἑρμηνείας φωτισθεῖσα,
οὕτως δὴ καὶ ὁ νόμος ἐπληρώθη τοῦ εὐαγγελίου
    φωτισθέντος,   275
    καὶ ὁ λαὸς ἐκενώθη τῆς ἐκκλησίας ἀνασταθείσης·
καὶ ὁ τύπος ἐλύθη τοῦ κυρίου φανερωθέντος,
    καὶ σήμερον γέγονεν τά ποτε τίμια ἄτιμα
        τῶν φύσει τιμίων φανερωθέντων.

44 Ἦν γάρ ποτε τίμιος ἡ τοῦ προβάτου σφαγή,   280
    νῦν δὲ ἄτιμος διὰ τὴν τοῦ κυρίου ζωήν·
τίμιος ὁ τοῦ προβάτου θάνατος,
    νῦν δὲ ἄτιμος διὰ τὴν τοῦ κυρίου σωτηρίαν·
τίμιον τὸ τοῦ προβάτου αἷμα,
    νῦν δὲ ἄτιμον διὰ τὸ τοῦ κυρίου πνεῦμα·   285
τίμιος ἄφωνος ἀμνός,
    νῦν δὲ ἄτιμος διὰ τὸν ἄμωμον υἱόν·
τίμιος ὁ κάτω ναός,
    νῦν δὲ ἄτιμος διὰ τὸν ἄνω Χριστόν.

45 ἦν τίμιος ἡ κάτω Ἰερουσαλήμ,   290
    νῦν δὲ ἄτιμος διὰ τὴν ἄνω Ἰερουσαλήμ·
ἦν τίμιος ἡ στενὴ κληρονομία,
    νῦν δὲ ἄτιμος διὰ τὴν πλατεῖαν χάριν.

273 ὁ τύπος κενοῦται: κενοῦται ὁ τύπος
274 πληροῦται: κενοῦται   ὑπὸ: διὰ
286 τίμιος ἄφωνος: τίμιος ὁ ἄφωνος
290 ἦν: om.   292 ἦν: om.

42　But when the Church arose and the gospel came to be,
　　　　the type, depleted, gave up meaning to the truth:
　　　　and the law, fulfilled, gave up meaning to the gospel.

43　In the same way that the type is depleted,
　　　　conceding the image to what is intrinsically real,
　　　　and the analogy is brought to completion through the
　　　　　　elucidation of interpretation,
　　　so the law is fulfilled by the elucidation of the gospel,
　　　　and the people is depleted by the arising of the Church,
　　　and the model is dissolved by the appearance of the Lord.
　　　　And today those things of value are worthless,
　　　　since the things of true worth have been revealed.

44　For then the slaughter of the sheep was of value,
　　　　now it is worthless because of the Lord's life.
　　　The death of the sheep was of value,
　　　　now it is worthless because of the Lord's salvation.
　　　The blood of the sheep was of value
　　　　now it is worthless because of the Lord's Spirit.
　　　The dumb lamb was of value,
　　　　now it is worthless because of the son without spot.
　　　The temple below was of value,
　　　　now it is worthless because of the heavenly Christ.

45　The Jerusalem below was of value,
　　　　now it is worthless because of the heavenly Jerusalem.
　　　Once the narrow inheritance was of value,
　　　　now it is worthless because of the breadth of grace.

οὐ γὰρ ἐφ᾽ ἑνὶ τόπῳ οὐδὲ ἐν βραχεῖ σχοινίσματι
    ἡ τοῦ θεοῦ δόξα καθίδρυται,   295
ἀλλ᾽ ἐπὶ πάντα τὰ πέρατα τῆς οἰκουμένης
    ἐκκέχυται ἡ χάρις αὐτοῦ,
καὶ ἐνταῦθα κατεσκήνωκεν ὁ παντοκράτωρ θεός
    διὰ Χριστοῦ Ἰησοῦ·
ᾧ ἡ δόξα εἰς τοὺς αἰῶνας. ἀμήν.   300

46 Τὸ μὲν οὖν διήγημα τοῦ τύπου καὶ τῆς ἀνταποδόσεως
    ἀκηκόατε·
    ἀκούσατε καὶ τὴν κατασκευὴν τοῦ μυστηρίου·
    τί ἐστιν τὸ πάσχα;
    ἀπὸ γὰρ τοῦ συμβεβηκότος τὸ ὄνομα κέκληται·
    ἀπὸ τοῦ παθεῖν τὸ πάσχειν.   305
    μάθετε οὖν τίς ὁ πάσχων,
        καὶ τίς ὁ τῷ πάσχοντι συμπαθῶν,

For it is not on one place, nor in a narrow plot, that the glory
  of God is established,
  but on all the ends of the earth.[15]
For his grace has been poured out
  and the almighty God has made his dwelling there.
Through Christ our Lord,
  to whom be the glory for ever and ever. Amen

46 You have heard the narrative of the type and its
    correspondence:
    hear now the confirmation of the mystery.[16]
    What is the Pascha?[17]
    It is called by its name because of what constitutes it:
    from "suffer" comes "suffering."[18]
    Therefore, learn who is the suffering one, and who shares in
        the suffering one's suffering,

[15]The polemic against the temple, whilst derived from Johannine tradition (note in particular Jn 2.19–21, which associates the true temple with the body of Christ), is particularly pointed here because the slaughter of the paschal lambs was restricted to the temple, whereas Melito is suggesting that the death of Christ has significance throughout the world.

[16]Narrative (*diēgēma*) and confirmation (*kataskeuē*) are two parts of a normal speech in the Greek world. Melito alerted us earlier to the *narratio*, and now informs us that its confirmation will follow. The confirmation was intended to show the true meaning, and veracity, of the preceding narrative. Melito follows the pattern of *diēgēma-kataskeuē*, but does not simply follow it woodenly. Note that the narrative is of the type, whereas the demonstration is of the reality which the type represented, that is to say the true foundation of the mystery is the salvation wrought in Christ. This may accord to the pattern of the paschal vigil of the Quartodecimans, with the fasting gathering in darkness concentrating on the old model of the Pascha (at the time at which the Jews are keeping festival) and the following festivity, probably at midnight, centering on the fulfillment wrought in Christ.

[17]Rhetorical questions were common enough in Asian Greek rhetoric; this question however at this point has a particular significance since it corresponds in the liturgical action to the point at which the questions are asked in the Jewish Passover, in keeping with the direction at Exodus 12.26.

[18]This line is untranslatable; the rendition here is that of Hall, *Melito of Sardis on Pascha*, 23. The line cannot be rendered into English because it depends on the similarity of the two, unrelated, words Pascha and *paschein*, the latter of which means "to suffer."

καὶ διὰ τί πάρεστιν ὁ κύριος ἐπὶ τῆς γῆς,
ἵνα τὸν πάσχοντα ἀμφιασάμενος
ἁρπάσῃ εἰς τὰ ὕψηλα τῶν οὐρανῶν.   310

47 Ὁ θεὸς ἐν ἀρχῇ ποιήσας τὸν οὐρανὸν καὶ τὴν γῆν
καὶ πάντα τὰ ἐν αὐτοῖς διὰ τοῦ λόγου,
ἀνεπλάσατο ἀπὸ τῆς γῆς τὸν ἄνθρωπον
καὶ ἰδίαν πνοὴν μετέδωκεν.
τοῦτον δὲ ἔθετο εἰς τὸν παράδεισον κατὰ ἀνατολὰς   315
ἐν Ἔδεμ ἐκεῖ τρυφᾶν,
τάδε αὐτῷ νομοθετήσας διὰ τῆς ἐντολῆς·
ἀπὸ παντὸς ξύλου βρώσει φάγετε,
ἀπὸ δὲ τοῦ ξύλου τοῦ γινώσκειν ἀγαθὸν καὶ πονηρὸν
οὐ φάγεσθε·   320
ᾗ δ᾽ ἂν ἡμέρᾳ φάγῃ
θανάτῳ ἀποθανῇ.

48 ὁ δὲ ἄνθρωπος φύσει δεκτικὸς ὢν ἀγαθοῦ καὶ πονηροῦ,
ὡσεὶ βῶλος γῆς ἑκατέρωθεν σπερμάτων,
ἐδέξατο τὸν ἐχθρὸν καὶ λίχνον σύμβουλον,   325
καὶ προσαψάμενος τοῦ ξύλου παρέβη τὴν ἐντολὴν
καὶ παρήκουσεν τοῦ θεοῦ.
ἐξεβλήθη γοῦν εἰς τοῦτον τὸν κόσμον
ὡς εἰς δεσμωτήριον καταδίκων.

49 Τούτου δὲ πολυχόου καὶ πολυχρονίου γενομένου,   330
διὰ τῆς τοῦ ξύλου γεύσεως διαλυθέντος
καὶ εἰς γῆν χωρήσαντος,
κατελείφθη ὑπ᾽ αὐτοῦ κληρονομία τοῖς τέκνοις αὐτοῦ·
κατέλιπεν γὰρ τοῖς τέκνοις κληρονομίαν

---

308 διὰ τί: διά τι   τῆς γῆς: τὴν γῆν
314 ἰδίαν πνοὴν: εἴδει ἀναπνοὴν   315 ἀνατολὰς: ἀνατολῆς
318 ξύλου βρόσει: ξύλου τοῦ ἐν τῷ παραδείσῳ βρόσει
321 φάγῃ φάγητε   322 ἀποθανῇ: ἀποθανεῖσθε
328 γοῦν: οὖν   331 διαλυθέντος: om.

and why the Lord is present on the earth to surround himself
     with the suffering one,
and take him to the heights of the heavens.

47 God, in the beginning,
       having made the heaven and the earth and all in them
          through the Word,
       formed humanity from the earth and shared his own
          breath.
    He set him in the garden in the east, in Eden,
       there to rejoice.
    There he laid down for him the law, through his
          commandment:
       "Eat food from all the trees in the garden
          yet eat not from the tree of the knowledge of good and
          evil;
       on the day that you eat you shall die."

48 The man was susceptible by nature of good and evil
       as a clod of earth may receive seed of either kind
    and he consented to the wicked and seductive counsellor,
       and stretched out for the tree and broke the commandment
          and disobeyed God.
    For this was he thrown out into this world, condemned as
          though to prison.

49 This man became fecund and long-lived,
       yet through tasting of the tree he was destroyed,
          and was dissolved into the earth.
    He left an inheritance to his children
       and as an inheritance he left his children:

οὐχ ἁγνείαν ἀλλὰ πορνείαν,   335
οὐκ ἀφθαρσίαν ἀλλὰ φθοράν,
οὐ τιμὴν ἀλλὰ ἀτιμίαν,
οὐκ ἐλευθερίαν ἀλλὰ δουλείαν,
οὐ βασιλείαν ἀλλὰ τυραννίδα,
οὐ ζωὴν ἀλλὰ θάνατον,   340
οὐ σωτηρίαν ἀλλὰ ἀπώλειαν.

50 καινὴ δὲ καὶ φοβερὰ ἡ τῶν ἀνθρώπων ἐπὶ τῆς γῆς ἐγίνετο
ἀπώλεια.
τάδε γὰρ συνέβαινεν αὐτοῖς·
    ἀνηρπάζοντο ὑπὸ τῆς τυραννικῆς ἁμαρτίας,
    καὶ ἤγοντο εἰς τοὺς χώρους τῶν ἐπιθυμιῶν   345
    ἐν οἷς περιηντλοῦντο ὑπὸ τῶν ἀκορέστων ἡδονῶν,
        ὑπὸ μοιχείας,
        ὑπὸ πορνείας,
        ὑπὸ ἀσελγείας,
        ὑπὸ φιλαργυρίας,   350
        ὑπὸ φόνων,
        ὑπὸ αἱμάτων,
        ὑπὸ τυραννίδος πονηρᾶς,
        ὑπὸ τυραννίδος παρανόμου.

51 καὶ γὰρ πατὴρ ἐπὶ υἱὸν ξίφος ἐπηνέγκατο,   355
καὶ υἱὸς πατρὶ χεῖρας προσήνεγκεν
καὶ μασθοὺς τιθηνοὺς ἀσεβὴς ἐτύπτησεν·
καὶ ἀδελφὸς ἀδελφὸν ἀπέκτεινεν,
καὶ ξένος ξένον ἠδίκησεν,
καὶ φίλος φίλον ἐφόνευσεν,   360
καὶ ἄνθρωπος ἄνθρωπον ἀπέσφαξεν τυραννικῇ δεξιᾷ.
πάντες οὖν οἱ μὲν ἀνθρωποκτόνοι,

349 ἀσελγείας: ἀσελγείας ἐπὶ ἐπιθυμίας
353 πονηρᾶς: πονηρίας   357 μασθοὺς: μαστοὺς
362 ἀνθρωποκτόνοι: ἀνθρωποκτόνοι, οἱ δὲ ἀδελφοκτόνοι

not purity but lust,
not incorruption but decay,
not honor but dishonor,
not freedom but bondage,
not sovereignty but tyranny,
not life but death,
not salvation but destruction.

50 Strange and terrible was the destruction of people on earth,
for these things attended them:
they were grasped by tyrannical sin
and they were led to the land of sensuality,
where they were swamped in unsatisfying pleasures:
by adultery,
by lust,
by license,
by love of money,
by murder,
by the shedding of blood,
by the tyranny of evil,
by the tyranny of lawlessness.

51 The father took up sword against his son
and the son laid hands upon his father
and impiously struck the breasts which fed him.
And brother killed brother,
and host harmed guest,
and friend murdered friend,
and man struck down man with a tyrannical right hand.
Everyone became murderers,

οἱ δὲ πατροκτόνοι,
οἱ δὲ τεκνοκτόνοι,
οἱ δὲ ἀδελφοκτόνοι ἐπὶ τῆς γῆς ἐγενήθησαν.   365

52 τὸ δὲ καινότερον καὶ φοβερώτερον ἐπὶ τῆς γῆς ηὑρίσκετο·
μήτηρ τις ἥπτετο σαρκῶν ὧν ἐγέννησεν,
καὶ προσήπτετο ὧν ἐξέθρεψεν μασθοῖς,
καὶ τὸν καρπὸν τῆς κοιλίας εἰς κοιλίαν κατώρυσσεν,
καὶ φοβερὸς τάφος ἐγίνετο ἡ δυστυχὴς μήτηρ,   370
ὃ ἐκύησεν καταπίνουσα τέκνον ουκετι προσλαλουν.

53 πολλὰ δὲ καὶ ἕτερα, ξένα καὶ φοβερώτερα καὶ ἀσελγέστερα,
    ἐν τοῖς ἀνθρώποις ηὑρίσκετο·
    πατὴρ ἐπὶ παιδὸς κοίτην,
    καὶ υἱὸς ἐπὶ μητρός,   375
    καὶ ἀδελφὸς ἐπὶ ἀδελφῆς,
    καὶ ἄρρην ἐπὶ ἄρρενος,
    καὶ ἕτερος ἐπὶ τὴν γυναῖκα τοῦ πλησίον ἐχρεμέτιζον.

54 Ἐπὶ δὲ τούτοις ἡ ἁμαρτία ηὐφραίνετο,
    ἣ τοῦ θανάτου σύνεργος ὑπάρχουσα   380
    προοδοιπορει εις τας των ανθρωπων ψυχάς,
    καὶ ἑτοιμάζει αὐτῷ τροφὰς τὰ τῶν νεκρῶν σώματα.
    εἰς πᾶσαν δὲ ψυχὴν ἐτίθει ἡ ἁμαρτία ἴχνος
    καὶ εἰς οὓς ἂν ἔθηκεν τούτους ἔδει τελευτᾶν.

55 πᾶσα οὖν σὰρξ ὑπὸ ἁμαρτίαν ἔπιπτεν   385
    καὶ πᾶν σῶμα ὑπὸ θάνατον,
    καὶ πᾶσα ψυχὴ ἐκ τοῦ σαρκίνου οἴκου ἐξηλαύνετο.

365 οἱ δὲ ἀδελφοκτόνοι: om.
366 καινότερον καὶ φοβερώτερον: φοβερώτερον καὶ καινότερον
    τῆς γῆς: om.
368 καὶ: om.   μασθοὺς: μαστοὺς   378 ἕτερος: ἑκάτερος
381 προοδοιπορεῖ: προωδοιπορεῖ

parricides,
infanticides,
fratricides, everyone on earth.[19]

52 The strangest and most terrible thing happened on the earth:
    a mother touched the flesh which she had borne
    and fastened onto those she had fed at the breast;
    and the fruit of her loins she received in her loins
    becoming a terrible tomb, the wretched mother
    gobbling up, not gabbling to, what she had borne.

53 Many other bizarre and most terrible and dissolute things
    took place among people:
    a father went to bed with his child,
    a son with his mother,
    and a brother with his sister and a male with a male,
    and each was braying for his neighbor's wife.

54 Sin rejoiced in all of this,
    working together with death,
    making forays into human souls
    and preparing the bodies of the dead as his food.
    Sin set his sign on every one
    and those on whom he etched his mark were doomed to
        death.

55 All flesh fell under sin,
    and every body under death,
    and every soul was plucked from its dwelling of flesh,

[19]Both scriptural narratives and Greek mythology provide the basis for this account. As a decline narrative it is a typical device of rhetoricians and philosophers of the period. We may compare in particular Ps.-Anacharsis, *Letter* 9: "Long ago the earth was the common possession of god and of people. In time however they transgressed, dedicating to the Gods as their own territory what was the common possession of all. The gods, in return for this, gave fitting gifts in return: strife, desire for pleasure, meanness of spirit. As these things mixed and separated there grew up all the evils which affect all mortals. . . . "

καὶ τὸ λημφθὲν ἐκ γῆς εἰς γῆν ἀνελύετο,
  καὶ τὸ δωρηθὲν ἐκ θεοῦ εἰς ᾅδην κατεκλείετο·
καὶ λύσις ἐγίνετο τῆς καλῆς ἁρμογῆς,   390
  καὶ διεχωρίζετο τὸ καλὸν σῶμα.

56 ἦν γὰρ ὁ ἄνθρωπος ὑπὸ τοῦ θανάτου μεριζόμενος.
    καινὴ γὰρ συμφορὰ καὶ ἅλωσις περιεῖχεν αὐτόν,
    καὶ εἵλκετο αἰχμάλωτος ὑπὸ τὰς τοῦ θανάτου σκιάς,
    ἔκειτο δὲ ἔρημος ἡ τοῦ πατρὸς εἰκών.   395
    διὰ ταύτην οὖν τὴν αἰτίαν τὸ τοῦ πάσχα μυστήριον
      τετέλεσται ἐν τῷ τοῦ κυρίου σώματι.

57 Πρότερον δὲ ὁ κύριος προῳκονόμησεν τὰ ἑαυτοῦ πάθη
      ἐν πατριάρχαις καὶ ἐν προφήταις καὶ ἐν παντὶ τῷ λαῷ,
    διά τε νόμου καὶ προφητῶν ἐπισφραγισάμενος.   400
    τὸ γὰρ μέλλον καινῶς καὶ μεγάλως ἔσεσθαι,
      τοῦτο ἐκ μακροῦ προοικονομεῖται,
    ἵν’ ὁπόταν γένηται πίστεως τύχῃ
      ἐκ μακροῦ προοραθέν.

58 οὕτω δὴ καὶ τὸ τοῦ κυρίου μυστήριον   405
      ἐκ μακροῦ προτυπωθέν,
        διὰ δὲ τύπον ὁραθέν,
      σήμερον πίστεως τυγχάνει τετελεσμένον
        καίτοι ὡς καινὸν τοῖς ἀνθρώποις νομιζόμενον.
    ἔστιν γὰρ καινὸν καὶ παλαιὸν τὸ τοῦ κυρίου μυστήριον·   410
      παλαιὸν μὲν κατὰ τὸν νόμον,
        καινὸν δὲ κατὰ τὴν χάριν.
    ἀλλ’ ἐὰν ἀποβλέψῃς εἰς τὸν τύπον,
      τοῦτον ὄψῃ διὰ τῆς ἐκβάσεως.

---

394 καὶ: om.   οὖν: γοῦν   407 διὰ δὲ τύπον: om.
408 σήμερον: δὲ σήμερον   410 καινὸν καὶ παλαιὸν: παλαιὸν καὶ καινὸν
411 νόμον: τύπον   414 ὄψῃ: ὄψῃ τὸ ἀληθὲς

and that which was taken from the dust was reduced to dust,
    and the gift of God was locked away in Hades.
What was marvelously knit together was unraveled,
    and the beautiful body divided.

56 Humanity was doled out by death
    for a strange disaster and captivity surrounded him;
    he was dragged off a captive under the shadow of death
    and the Father's image was left desolate.
For this reason is the paschal mystery completed
    in the body of the Lord.

57 The Lord made advance preparation for his own suffering
    in the patriarchs and in the prophets and in the whole
       people;
    through the law and the prophets he sealed them.
That which more recently and most excellently came to pass
    he arranged from of old.
For when it would come to pass it would find faith,
    having been foreseen of old.[20]

58 Thus the mystery of the Lord,
    prefigured from of old through the vision of a type,
       is today fulfilled and has found faith,
    even though people think it something new.
For the mystery of the Lord is both new and old;
    old with respect to the law
       but new with respect to grace.
But if you scrutinize the type through its outcome you will
    discern him.

---

[20]Cf. Justin, *First Apology* 33.2.

59 τοιγαροῦν εἰ βούλει τὸ τοῦ κυρίου μυστήριον ἰδέσθαι,   415
    ἀπόβλεψον εἰς τὸν Ἀβὲλ τὸν ὁμοίως φονευόμενον,
       εἰς τὸν Ἰσὰκ τὸν ὁμοίως συμποδιζόμενον,
       εἰς τὸν Ἰωσὴφ τὸν ὁμοίως πιπρασκόμενον,
       εἰς τὸν Μωυσέα τὸν ὁμοίως ἐκτιθέμενον,
       εἰς τὸν Δαυεὶδ τὸν ὁμοίως διωκόμενον,   420
       εἰς τοὺς προφήτας τοὺς ὁμοίως διὰ Χριστὸν πάσχοντας.

60 ἀπόβλεψον δὲ καὶ εἰς τὸ ἐν γῇ Αἰγύπτῳ πρόβατον
    σφαζόμενον,
       τὸ πάταξαν τὴν Αἴγυπτον
       καὶ σῶσαν τὸν Ἰσραὴλ διὰ τοῦ αἵματος.

61 Ἔστιν δὲ διὰ προφητικῆς φωνῆς τὸ τοῦ κυρίου μυστήριον
    κηρυσσόμενον.   425
       φησὶν γὰρ Μωυσῆς πρὸς τὸν λαόν·
       Καὶ ὄψεσθε τὴν ζωὴν ὑμῶν κρεμαμένην
          ἔμπροσθεν τῶν ὀφθαλμῶν ὑμῶν νυκτὸς καὶ ἡμέρας,
       καὶ οὐ μὴ πιστεύσητε ἐπὶ τὴν ζωὴν ὑμῶν.

62 ὁ δὲ Δαυεὶδ εἶπεν·   430
       Ἵνα τί ἐφρύαξαν ἔθνη
          καὶ λαοὶ ἐμελέτησαν κενά;
       παρέστησαν οἱ βασιλεῖς τῆς γῆς
          καὶ οἱ ἄρχοντες συνήχθησαν ἐπὶ τὸ αὐτὸ
       κατὰ τοῦ κυρίου καὶ κατὰ τοῦ χριστοῦ αὐτοῦ.   435

63 ὁ δὲ Ἰερεμίας.
       ἐγὼ ὡς ἄρνιον ἄκακον ἀγόμενον τοῦ θύεσθαι.
       ἐλογίσαντο εἰς ἐμὲ κακὰ εἰπόντες·

---

415 ἀπόβλεψον εἰς: ἀπόβλεψον δὴ εἰς
421 διὰ Χριστὸν: διὰ τὸν Χριστὸν   τὸ πάταξαν: τὸν πατάξαντα   τὴν: om.
424 σῶσαν: σωσάντα

59 Thus if you wish to see the mystery of the Lord
    look at Abel who is likewise slain,
        at Isaac who is likewise tied up,[21]
        at Joseph who is likewise traded,
        at Moses who is likewise exposed,
        at David who is likewise hunted down,
        at the prophets who likewise suffer for the sake of Christ.

60 And look at the sheep, slaughtered in the land of Egypt,
        which saved Israel through its blood whilst Egypt was
            struck down.

61 The Mystery of the Lord is proclaimed through the prophetic
    voice.
    For Moses says to the people:
        "And you shall look upon your life hanging before your
            eyes night and day, and you will not have faith in your
            life."[22]

62 David says:
        "Why have the nations been haughty, and the peoples
            imagined vain things?
        The kings of the earth stood by and the rulers gathered
            themselves together
        against the Lord and against his anointed one."[23]

63 Jeremiah says:
        "I am like a harmless lamb led to sacrifice;
        they planned evil for me saying: come let us put wood on

---

[21]There is a tradition in Judaism concerning Isaac's sacrifice as a redemptive offering; it is possible to perceive an allusion to this here, where Isaac's suffering is seen as a type of that of Christ. See fragments 9–11 below for further discussion and bibliography.

[22]Deut 28.66.

[23]Ps 2.1–2.

Δεῦτε ἐμβάλωμεν ξύλον εἰς τὸν ἄρτον αὐτοῦ
καὶ ἐκτρίψωμεν αὐτὸν ἐκ γῆς ζώντων·   440
καὶ τὸ ὄνομα αὐτοῦ οὐ μὴ μνησθῇ.

64 ὁ δὲ Ἠσαίας·
Ὡς πρόβατον εἰς σφαγὴν ἤχθη,
καὶ ὡς ἀμνὸς ἄφωνος ἐναντίον τοῦ κείραντος αὐτόν
οὗτος οὐκ ἀνοίγει τὸ στόμα αὐτοῦ·   445
τὴν δὲ γενεὰν αὐτοῦ τίς διηγήσεται;

65 πολλὰ μὲν οὖν καὶ ἕτερα ὑπὸ πολλῶν προφητῶν ἐκηρύχθη
εἰς τὸ τοῦ πάσχα μυστήριον,
ὅ ἐστιν Χριστός·
ᾧ ἡ δόξα εἰς τοὺς αἰῶνας. ἀμήν.   450

66 Οὗτος ἀφικόμενος ἐξ οὐρανῶν ἐπὶ τὴν γῆν διὰ τὸν πάσχοντα,
αὐτὸν δὲ ἐκεῖνον ἐνδυσάμενος διὰ παρθένου μήτρας
καὶ προελθὼν ἄνθρωπος,

443 εἰς: ἐπὶ
446 δὲ: om.
447 οὖν: om.

his bread and let us rub him out from the land of the
living; and his name shall not be remembered."[24]

64   Isaiah says:
  "Like a sheep he was led to slaughter and like a silent lamb
    before its shearer he does not open his mouth; who shall
    tell of his generation?"[25]

65   Many other things were proclaimed by many prophets
  concerning the mystery of the Pascha, who is Christ,
    to whom be the glory for ever.
    Amen.[26]

66   This is the one who comes from heaven onto the earth by
  means of the suffering one,
  and wraps himself in the suffering one by means of a virgin
    womb,[27]

---

[24]Jer 11.19.

[25]Is 53.7–8. Note that this collection of proof-texts stands at the conclusion of
what is effectively the *probatio* of Melito's declaration and thus contributes to the proof
by means of citation; this procedure is typical of the schools, but is also consonant
with the practice of Christian prophecy, where every prophecy required proof, which
might be supplied by showing it to be consonant with the Scriptures. It is possible that
these prophetic Scriptures had been read at the paschal vigil.

[26]With this doxology the *probatio* ends. Melito has shown how good and right it
is that in the mercy of God the Pascha should be kept. He now turns to his *peroratio*,
bringing together all the themes of his discourse, praising God, and making the salvation worked by God at Pascha a reality for his audience.

[27]The word for suffering is here *paschōn*. The connection is being made still
between Jesus and the paschal lamb. This is particularly significant in that the word
used for Jesus' coming is *aphikomenos*. This is reminiscent of the word *aphikoman*, a
portion of bread broken off from the main loaf at the Passover seder of Judaism, and
hidden. In modern Judaism the finding of the *aphikoman* is considered a children's
game, but according to Daube the *aphikoman* was originally a messianic symbol, and
was intended to indicate the coming of the Messiah. Here the identification of *aphikoman* and Jesus as Messiah are tied together; we may suggest moreover that here begins
the liturgical climax, and that at this point in the seder the *aphikoman* is revealed,
identified with the Messiah, with Jesus and through Jesus with the paschal lamb. See in
particular on this David Daube, *He That Cometh* (London: Diocese of London, 1966).

άπεδέξατο τὰ τοῦ πάσχοντος πάθη
    διὰ τοῦ παθεῖν δυναμένου σώματος,   455
    καὶ κατέλυσεν τὰ τῆς σαρκὸς πάθη·
    τῷ δὲ θανεῖν μὴ δυναμένῳ πνεύματι
    ἀπέκτεινεν τὸν ἀνθρωποκτόνον θάνατον.

67 αὐτὸς γὰρ ὡς ἀμνὸς ἀχθεὶς
    καὶ ὡς πρόβατον σφαγείς,   460
    ἐλυτρώσατο ἡμᾶς ἐκ τῆς τοῦ κόσμου λατρείας
    ὡς ἐκ γῆς Αἰγύπτου,
    καὶ ἔλυσεν ἐκ τῆς τοῦ διαβόλου δουλείας
    ὡς ἐκ χειρὸς Φαραώ,
    καὶ ἐσφράγισεν ἡμῶν τὰς ψυχὰς τῷ ἰδίῳ πνεύματι   465
    καὶ τὰ μέλη τοῦ σώματος τῷ ἰδίῳ αἵματι.

68 οὗτός ἐστιν ὁ τὸν θάνατον ἐνδύσας αἰσχύνην
    καὶ τὸν διάβολον στήσας πενθήρη
    ὡς Μωυσῆς τὸν Φαραώ.
    οὗτός ἐστιν ὁ τὴν ἀνομίαν πατάξας   470
    καὶ τὴν ἀδικίαν ἀτεκνώσας
    ὡς Μωυσῆς Αἴγυπτον.
    οὗτός ἐστιν ὁ ῥυσάμενος ἡμᾶς ἐκ δουλείας εἰς ἐλευθερίαν,
    ἐκ σκότους εἰς φῶς,
    ἐκ θανάτου εἰς ζωήν,   475
    ἐκ τυραννίδος εἰς βασιλείαν αἰώνιαν,

463 ἔλευσεν: ἔλευσεν ἡμᾶς

and comes forth a human being.
He accepted the suffering of the suffering one
   through suffering in a body which could suffer,
and set free the flesh from suffering.
Through the Spirit which cannot die
   he slew the manslayer death.

67 He is the one led like a lamb
   and slaughtered like a sheep;
   he ransomed us from the worship of the world
     as from the land of Egypt,
   and he set us free from the slavery of the devil
     as from the hand of Pharaoh,
   and sealed our souls with his own Spirit,
     and the members of our body with his blood.[28]

68 This is the one who clad death in shame
   and, as Moses did to Pharaoh,
     made the devil grieve.
This is the one who struck down lawlessness
   and made injustice childless,
     as Moses did to Egypt.
This is the one who delivered us from slavery to freedom,
     from darkness into light,
     from death into life,
     from tyranny into an eternal Kingdom,[29]

[28]Note the association of the spirit and the blood of Christ, similar to that made by Apollinarius, Melito's Asian contemporary, who identifies the water and the blood which flowed from the side of Christ with his word and his spirit (see the citation from Apollinarius at pp. 105–106 below; note also 1 Jn 5.6–8). It would be mistaken to see a reference to baptism here, for although there is some baptismal language, such as the references to sealing with the blood of the lamb, the fact that according to Melito the doorposts are "anointed," and the shedding of blood "illuminates" Israel, this is imagery and does not imply that baptism occurred at this liturgical occasion. On the matter of paschal baptism see S. G. Hall, "Paschal Baptism," *Studia Evangelica* 6, Texte und Untersuchungen 112 (Berlin: Akademie, 1973), 239–51.

[29]The close similarity between this passage and Mishnah *Pesahim* 10.5, which is part of the paschal haggadah, is particularly significant. This was one of the parallels

καὶ ποιήσας ἡμᾶς ἱεράτευμα καινὸν
καὶ λαὸν περιούσιον αἰώνιον.

69 οὗτός ἐστιν τὸ πάσχα τῆς σωτηρίας ἡμῶν.

οὗτός ἐστιν ὁ ἐν πολλοῖς πολλὰ ὑπομείνας·   480
οὗτός ἐστιν ὁ ἐν τῷ Ἀβὲλ φονευθείς,
    ἐν δὲ τῷ Ἰσὰκ δεθείς,
    ἐν δὲ τῷ Ἰακὼβ ξενιτεύσας,
    ἐν δὲ τῷ Ἰωσὴφ πραθείς,
    ἐν δὲ τῷ Μωυσῇ ἐκτεθείς,   485
    ἐν δὲ τῷ ἀμνῷ σφαγείς,
    ἐν δὲ τῷ Δαυεὶδ διωχθείς,
    ἐν δὲ τοῖς προφήταις ἀτιμασθείς.

70 οὗτός ἐστιν ὁ ἐν παρθένῳ σαρκωθείς,
    ὁ ἐπὶ ξύλου κρεμασθείς,   490
    ὁ εἰς γῆν ταφείς,
    ὁ ἐκ νεκρῶν ἀνασταθείς,
    ὁ εἰς τὰ ὑψηλὰ τῶν οὐρανῶν ἀναλημφθείς.

71 οὗτός ἐστιν ὁ ἀμνὸς φονευόμενος·
οὗτός ἐστιν ὁ ἀμνὸς ὁ ἄφωνος·   495
οὗτός ἐστιν ὁ τεχθεὶς ἐκ Μαρίας τῆς καλῆς ἀμνάδος·
ουτος εστιν ο εξ αγελης λημφθείς,
    καὶ εἰς σφαγὴν συρείς,
    καὶ ἑσπέρας τυθείς,
    καὶ νύκτωρ ταφείς,   500
    ὁ ἐπὶ ξύλου μὴ συντριβείς,

494 φονευόμενος: ἄφωνος
495 ἄφωνος: φονευόμενος

and made us a new priesthood,
  and a people everlasting for himself.

69 This is the Pascha of our salvation:
  this is the one who in many people endured many things.
  This is the one who was murdered in Abel,
    tied up in Isaac,
    exiled in Jacob,
    sold in Joseph,
    exposed in Moses,
    slaughtered in the lamb,
    hunted down in David,
    dishonored in the prophets.

70 This is the one made flesh in a virgin,
    who was hanged on a tree,
    who was buried in the earth,
    who was raised from the dead,
    who was exalted to the heights of heaven.[30]

71 This is the lamb slain,
  this is the speechless lamb,
  this is the one born of Mary the fair ewe,
  this is the one taken from the flock,
    and led to slaughter.
    Who was sacrificed in the evening,
    and buried at night;
    who was not broken on the tree,

which first alerted scholars to the possibility that *On Pascha* might be a Christian Paschal haggadah. The passage from Mishnah *Pesahim* runs: He brought us out from bondage to freedom, from sorrow to gladness and from mourning to a festival day, and from darkness to a great light and from tyranny to redemption. . . .

[30]This emphasis on the exalted Christ is again surely reminiscent of the Johannine tradition, not simply of the visions in Revelation but of the exaltation tradition underlying John's Gospel, where, throughout the farewell discourses Jesus talks of glorification without mentioning resurrection.

εἰς γῆν μὴ λυθείς,
ἐκ νεκρῶν ἀναστάς,
καὶ ἀναστήσας τὸν ἄνθρωπον ἐκ τῆς κάτω ταφῆς.

72 Οὗτος πεφόνευται·   505
καὶ ποῦ πεφόνευται; ἐν μέσῳ Ἰερουσαλήμ.
ὑπὸ τίνων; ὑπὸ τοῦ Ἰσραήλ.
διὰ τί; ὅτι τοὺς χωλοὺς αὐτῶν ἐθεράπευσεν
καὶ τοὺς λεπροὺς αὐτῶν ἐκαθάρισεν
   καὶ τοὺς τυφλοὺς αὐτῶν ἐφωταγώγησεν   510
   καὶ τοὺς νεκροὺς αὐτῶν ἀνέστησεν,
      διὰ τοῦτο ἀπέθανεν.
ποῦ γέγραπται ἐν νόμῳ καὶ ἐν προφήταις·
Ἀνταπέδωκάν μοι κακὰ ἀντὶ ἀγαθῶν
   καὶ ἀτεκνίαν τῇ ψυχῇ μου,   515
λογισάμενοι ἐπ' ἐμὲ κακὰ εἰπόντες·
Δήσωμεν τὸν δίκαιον
   ὅτι δύσχρηστος ἡμῖν ἐστιν;

507 Back-translation from Latin versions: om.

who was not undone in the earth,
who rose from the dead and resurrected humankind from
   the grave below.

72 This is the one who has been murdered.
And where murdered?
In the middle of Jerusalem.[31]
By whom? By Israel.[32]
Why? Because he healed their lame,
and cleansed their lepers,
   and enlightened their blind,
   and raised up their dead;
      and therefore he died.
Where is it written in the law and the prophets:
   "They repaid me bad things for good and childlessness for
      my soul.
   They planned wickedness for me saying:
   'Let us tie up the just man because he is a nuisance to us'?"

---

[31] Although it has been argued (by A. E. Harvey, "Melito and Jerusalem," *Journal of Theological Studies* 17 [1966]: 401–40) that Melito places the crucifixion in the middle of Jerusalem, rather than outside the walls as the Gospels state, because the site of the crucifixion (now the Church of the Holy Sepulchre) was in the middle of Jerusalem after the resiting of the walls of the city early in the second century, this is more probably a theological statement resulting from the identification of the death of Christ with that of the lambs in the Temple. That Mount Moriah, where Isaac was offered, was subsequently identified in the Jewish tradition with the Temple mount, would tend to lend support to this interpretation. See also, on the rhetorical force of this situation, Urban C. Wahlde, "The References to the Time and Place of the Crucifixion in the *Peri Pascha* of Melito of Sardis," *Journal of Theological Studies* 60 (2009): 556–69.

[32] The manner in which Melito blames Israel entirely for the events of the passion, without mention of the Romans, is shared with the similarly Quartodeciman *Gospel of Peter*. Whereas Melito may be concerned not to alienate the Roman state, it is more probable that the blame of Israel derives from his Johannine theological tradition, whose social situation and need to distinguish itself from Judaism closely mirrors that of Melito himself. Post-Holocaust commentators have picked up strongly on Melito's anti-Judaism here. We should note however that the anti-Judaism is a counterpoint to the acts of God, and to the salvation of the Gentiles. Melito himself would not have identified it as a theme in his work, however prominent this section is in modern discussion. For further discussion and bibliography see the introduction.

73 τί ἐποίησας, ὦ Ἰσραήλ, τὸ καινὸν ἀδίκημα;
    ἠτίμησας τὸν τιμήσαντά σε·   520
    ἠδόξησας τὸν δοξάσαντά σε·
    ἀπηρνήσω τὸν ὁμολογήσαντά σε·
    ἀπεκήρυξας τὸν κηρύξαντά σε·
    ἀπέκτεινας τὸν ζωοποιήσαντά σε.

74 τί ἐποίησας, ὦ Ἰσραήλ; ἢ οὐ γέγραπταί σοι·   525
    Οὐκ ἐκχεεῖς αἷμα ἀθῷον,
        ἵνα μὴ θάνῃς κακῶς;
    Ἐγὼ μέν, φησὶν Ἰσραήλ, ἀπέκτεινα τὸν κύριον.
    διὰ τί; ὅτι ἔδει αὐτὸν ἀποθανεῖν.
    πεπλάνησαι, ὦ Ἰσραήλ, τοιαῦτα σοφιζόμενος   530
        ἐπὶ τῇ τοῦ κυρίου σφαγῇ.

75 ἔδει αὐτὸν παθεῖν, ἀλλ᾽ οὐχ ὑπὸ σοῦ·
    ἔδει αὐτὸν ἀτιμασθῆναι, ἀλλ᾽ οὐχ ὑπὸ σοῦ·
    ἔδει αὐτὸν κριθῆναι, ἀλλ᾽ οὐχ ὑπὸ σοῦ·
    ἔδει αὐτὸν κρεμασθῆναι, ἀλλ᾽ οὐχ ὑπὸ σοῦ   535
        τῆς δὲ σῆς δεξιᾶς.

76 ταύτην, ὦ Ἰσραήλ, πρὸς τὸν θεὸν ὤφειλες βοῆσαι τὴν φωνήν·
    Ὦ Δέσποτα, εἰ καὶ ἔδει σου τὸν υἱὸν παθεῖν
        καὶ τοῦτό σου τὸ θέλημα,
    πασχέτω δή, ἀλλὰ ὑπ᾽ ἐμοῦ μή·   540
    πασχέτω ὑπὸ ἀλλοφύλων,
    κρινέσθω ὑπὸ ἀκροβύστων,
    προσηλούσθω ὑπὸ τυραννικῆς δεξιᾶς,
        ὑπὸ δὲ ἐμοῦ μή.

527 θάνῃς: ἀποθάνῃς
529 ἀποθανεῖν: παθεῖν
535 σοῦ τῆς δὲ σῆς δεξιᾶς: τῆς δεξιᾶς σου
539 σου τὸ: σού ἐστιν τὸ

73 What strange injustice have you done, O Israel?
>You have dishonored the one who honored you,
>you have disgraced the one who glorified you,
>you have denied the one who owned you,
>you have ignored the one who made you known,
>you have murdered the one who gave you life.

74 O Israel, what have you done?
>Is it not written for you: "You shall not spill innocent blood"
>>so that you might not die the death of the wicked?
>
>"I," said Israel. "I killed the Lord."
>>Why? "Because he had to die."
>
>You have erred, O Israel, to reason so
>>about the slaughter of the Lord.

75 He had to suffer, but not through you.
>He had to be dishonored, but not by you.
>He had to be judged, but not by you.
>he had to be hung up, but not by you and by your right hand.

76 This, O Israel, is the cry with which you should have called to God:
>"O Master, if your Son should suffer,
>>and this is your will,
>
>let him suffer indeed, but not by me.
>Let him suffer through foreigners,
>let him be judged by the uncircumcised,
>let him be nailed in place by a tyrannical right hand,
>>not mine."

77 σὺ δὲ ταύτην, ὦ Ἰσραήλ, πρὸς τὸν θεὸν οὐκ ἐβόησας τὴν
    φωνήν,   545
    οὐδὲ ἀφωσίωσαι τῷ δεσπότῃ,
    οὐδὲ ἐδυσωπήθης τὰ ἔργα αὐτοῦ.

78 οὐκ ἐδυσώπησέν σε χεὶρ ξηρὰ ἀποκατασταθεῖσα τῷ σώματι,
    οὐδὲ ὀφθαλμοὶ πηρῶν διὰ χειρὸς ἀνοιγόμενοι,
    οὐδὲ λελυμένα σώματα διὰ φωνῆς ἀναπηγνύμενα.   550
    οὐδὲ τὸ καινότερόν σε ἐδυσώπησεν σημεῖον,
    νεκρὸς ἐκ μνημείου ἐγειρόμενος ἤδη τεσσάρων ἡμερῶν.

79 σὺ μὲν οὖν ταῦτα παραπεμψάμενος
    ἔσπευσας ἐπὶ τὴν τοῦ κυρίου σφαγήν.
    ἡτοίμασας αὐτῷ ἥλους ὀξεῖς καὶ μάρτυρας ψευδεῖς   555
    καὶ βρόχους καὶ μάστιγας
    καὶ ὄξος καὶ χολὴν
    καὶ μάχαιραν καὶ θλῖψιν ὡς ἐπὶ φόνιον λῃστήν.
    ἐπηνέγκω γὰρ αὐτοῦ καὶ μάστιγας τῷ σώματι
    καὶ ἄκανθαν τῇ κεφαλῇ αὐτοῦ·   560
    καὶ τὰς καλὰς αὐτοῦ χεῖρας ἔδησας
    αἵ σε ἔπλασαν ἀπὸ γῆς·
    καὶ τὸ καλὸν αὐτοῦ ἐκεῖνο στόμα τὸ ψωμίσαν σε ζωὴν
    ἐψώμισας χολήν.
    καὶ ἀπέκτεινάς σου τὸν κύριον ἐν τῇ μεγάλῃ ἑορτῇ.   565

548 ἀποκατασταθεῖσα: ἀποκαθεσταμένη
549 χειρὸς: χειρὸς αὐτοῦ
550 λελυμένα: παραλελυμένα   φωνῆς: φωνῆς αὐτοῦ
559 ἐπηνέγκω: ἐπενεγκὼν   αὐτοῦ: αὐτῷ

77 With this cry, O Israel, you did not call out to God.
>   Nor did you devote yourself to the master,
>   nor did you have regard for his works.

78 You did not have regard for the withered hand restored to its body,
>   nor the eyes of the maimed opened by a hand,
>   nor limp bodies made strong through a voice.
>   Nor did you regard the strangest of signs,
>   a corpse four days dead called alive from a tomb.[33]

79 You put these things to one side,
>   you hurried to the slaughter of the Lord.
>   You prepared for him sharp nails and false witnesses,
>   and ropes and whips,
>   and vinegar and gall,
>   and a sword and torture as against a murderous thief.
>   You brought forth a flogging for his body,
>   and thorns for his head;
>   and you bound his goodly hands,
>   which formed you from the earth.
>   And you fed with gall his goodly mouth which fed you with life.
>   And you killed your Lord at the great feast.[34]

---

[33] Melito's emphasis on the signs of Jesus' activity (*sēmeia*) is again reminiscent of the Johannine tradition.

[34] Technically this would mean the feast of unleavened bread, which was the day that followed the evening celebration of Passover. If this were the case then this would mean that Melito was following a synoptic Gospel chronology, which in turn would make Quartodeciman practice rather inconsistent. However, in Melito's time Jews referred to the Passover rather loosely as the "great feast," and did not make a close distinction between Passover and the following days of unleavened bread. For this reason too much should not be read into this statement. The festivities which are described are those of the Passover seder, and are by implication the same as those celebrated by Melito. For further details and references see *The Lamb's High Feast*, 148–49.

80 καὶ σὺ μὲν ἦσθα εὐφραινόμενος,
      ἐκεῖνος δὲ λιμώττων·
      σὺ ἔπινες οἶνον καὶ ἄρτον ἤσθιες,
      ἐκεῖνος δὲ ὄξος καὶ χολήν·
      σὺ ἦσθα φαιδρὸς τῷ προσώπῳ,   570
      ἐκεῖνος δὲ ἐσκυθρώπαζεν·
      σὺ ἦσθα ἀγαλλιώμενος,
      ἐκεῖνος δὲ ἐθλίβετο·
      σὺ ἔψαλλες,
      ἐκεῖνος δὲ ἐκρίνετο·   575
      σὺ ἐκέλευες,
      ἐκεῖνος δὲ προσηλοῦτο·
      σὺ ἐχόρευες,
      ἐκεῖνος δὲ ἐθάπτετο·
      σὺ μὲν ἐπὶ στρωμνῆς μαλακῆς ἦσθα κατακείμενος,   580
      ἐκεῖνος δὲ ἐν τάφῳ καὶ σορῷ.

81 Ὦ Ἰσραὴλ παράνομε, τί τοῦτο ἀπηργάσω τὸ καινὸν ἀδίκημα,
      καινοῖς ἐμβαλών σου τὸν κύριον πάθεσιν,
      τὸν δεσπότην σου,
      τὸν πλάσαντά σε,   585
      τὸν ποιήσαντά σε,
      τὸν τιμήσαντά σε,
      τὸν Ἰσραήλ σε καλέσαντα;

82 σὺ δὲ Ἰσραὴλ οὐχ εὑρέθης·
      οὐ γὰρ εἶδες τὸν θεόν,   590
      οὐκ ἐνόησας τὸν κύριον·
      οὐκ ᾔδεις, ὦ Ἰσραήλ,
      ὅτι οὗτός ἐστιν ὁ πρωτότοκος τοῦ θεοῦ,
      ὁ πρὸ ἑωσφόρου γεννηθείς,

582 τί: τί δὴ
588 σε καλέσαντα: καλέσαντά σε

80　And while you were rejoicing he was starving.
　　　You were drinking wine and eating bread;
　　　　he had vinegar and gall.
　　　Your face was bright whereas his was cast down.
　　　You were triumphant while he was afflicted.
　　　You were making music while he was being judged.
　　　You were proposing toasts;
　　　　he was being nailed in place.
　　　You were dancing, he was buried.
　　　You were reclining on a cushioned couch,
　　　　he in grave and coffin.[35]

81　O lawless Israel, what is this new injustice you have done,
　　　casting strange sufferings on your Lord?
　　　　Your master who formed you,
　　　　who made you,
　　　　who honored you,
　　　　who called you "Israel."

82　You were not Israel.
　　You did not see God.[36]
　　You did not perceive the Lord, Israel,
　　　you did not recognize the first-born of God,
　　　　begotten before the morning star,

---

[35]This description of the Jewish celebration is perhaps also as much a picture of the Christian celebration. Note that bread and wine are singled out as the foods enjoyed, that the haggadah could be interpreted as the proposal of a toast, and that dancing was known in the Christian tradition, having particular prominence in *The Acts of John* (so W. C. van Unnik, "A Note on the Dance of Jesus in the *Acts of John*," *Vigiliae Christianae* 18 [1964]: 1–5).

[36]The interpretation of "Israel" to mean "the one who sees God" is found in Philo, *On the Change of Names* 81 and is implied in Jn 1.45–51.

ὁ τὸ φῶς ἐπανθίσας,   595
ὁ τὴν ἡμέραν λαμπρύνας,
ὁ τὸ σκότος διακρίνας,
ὁ τὴν πρώτην βαλβῖδα πήξας,
ὁ κρεμάσας τὴν γῆν,
ὁ σβέσας ἄβυσσον,   600
ὁ ἐκτείνας τὸ στερέωμα,
ὁ κοσμήσας τὸν κόσμον,
ὁ τοὺς ἐν οὐρανῷ ἁρμόσας ἀστέρας,
ὁ τοὺς φωστῆρας λαμπρύνας,
ὁ τοὺς ἐν οὐρανῷ ποιήσας ἀγγέλους,   605
ὁ τοὺς ἐκεῖ πήξας θρόνους,
ὁ τὸν ἐπὶ γῆς ἀναπλασάμενος ἄνθρωπον.

83 οὗτος ἦν ὁ ἐκλεξάμενός σε καὶ καθοδηγήσας σε
        ἀπὸ τοῦ Ἀδὰμ ἐπὶ τὸν Νῶε,
        ἀπὸ τοῦ Νῶε ἐπὶ τὸν Ἀβραάμ,   610
        ἀπὸ τοῦ Ἀβραὰμ ἐπὶ τὸν Ἰσὰκ
            καὶ τὸν Ἰακὼβ καὶ τοὺς ιβ πατριάρχας.

84 οὗτος ἦν ὁ καθοδηγήσας σε εἰς Αἴγυπτον,
        καὶ διαφυλάξας σε κἀκεῖ διαθρεψάμενος.
    οὗτος ἦν ὁ φωταγωγήσας σε ἐν στύλῳ   615
        καὶ σκεπάσας σε ἐν νεφέλῃ,
        ὁ τεμὼν Ἐρυθρὰν καὶ διαγαγών σε
        καὶ τὸν ἐχθρόν σου ἀπολέσας.

85 οὗτός ἐστιν ὁ ἐξ οὐρανοῦ σε μαννοδοτήσας,
        ὁ ἐκ πέτρας σε ποτίσας,   620
        ὁ ἐν Χωρὴβ σοι νομοθετήσας,
        ὁ ἐν γῇ σοι κληροδοτήσας,
        ὁ ἐξαποστείλας σοι τοὺς προφήτας,
        ὁ ἐγείρας σου τοὺς βασιλεῖς.

595 ἐπανθίσας: ἐπανεστήσας   617 Ἐρυθρὰν: Ἐρυθρὰν θάλασσαν
618 ἀπολέσας: ἀποσκεδάσας   619 μαννοδοτήσας: μανναδοτήσας Hall

who adorned the light,
who lit up the day,
who divided the darkness,
who fixed the first boundary,
who hung the earth,
who tamed the abyss,
who stretched out the firmament,
who furnished the world,
who arranged the stars in the heavens,
who lit up the great lights,
who made the angels in heaven,
who there established thrones,
who formed humanity on the earth.

83   It was he who chose you and led you,
from Adam to Noah,
from Noah to Abraham,
from Abraham to Isaac and Jacob and the twelve
patriarchs.

84   He it was who led you into Egypt,
and guarded you there and sustained you.
He it was who lit up your way with a pillar,
and sheltered you with a cloud.
He cut the Red Sea open, leading you through,
and destroyed the enemy.

85   He it is who gave you manna from heaven,
who gave you drink from a rock,
who gave you the law at Horeb,
who gave you the inheritance in the land,
who sent you the prophets,
who raised up kings for you.

86 οὗτός ἐστιν ὁ πρός σε ἀφικόμενος,   625
        ὁ τοὺς πάσχοντάς σου θεραπεύσας
        καὶ τοὺς νεκρούς σου ἀναστήσας.
        οὗτός ἐστιν εἰς ὃν ἐτόλμησας·
        οὗτός ἐστιν εἰς ὃν ἠσέβησας·
        οὗτός ἐστιν εἰς ὃν ἠδίκησας·   630
        οὗτός ἐστιν ὃν ἀπέκτεινας·
        οὗτός ἐστιν ὃν ἠργυρίσω
        ἀπαιτήσας παρ' αὐτοῦ τὸ δίδραχμα ὑπὲρ τῆς κεφαλῆς
        αὐτοῦ.

87 Ἀχάριστε Ἰσραήλ, δεῦρο καὶ κρίθητι πρὸς ἐμὲ
        περὶ τῆς ἀχαριστίας σου.   635
        πόσου ἀνετιμήσω τὸ ὑπ' αὐτοῦ πλασθῆναι;
        πόσου ἀνετιμήσω τὴν τῶν πατέρων σου ἀνεύρεσιν;
        πόσου ἀνετιμήσω τὴν εἰς Αἴγυπτον κάθοδον
        καὶ τὴν ἐκεῖ διατροφὴν διὰ τοῦ καλοῦ Ἰωσήφ;

88 πόσου ἀνετιμήσω τὰς δέκα πληγάς;   640
        πόσου ἀνετιμήσω τὸν νυκτερινὸν στῦλον
        καὶ τὴν ἡμερινὴν νεφέλην
        καὶ τὴν δι' Ἐρυθρᾶς διάβασιν;
        πόσου ἀνετιμήσω τὴν ἐξ οὐρανοῦ μαννοδοσίαν
        καὶ ἐκ πέτρας ὑδροπαροχίαν   645
        καὶ ἐν Χωρὴβ νομοθεσίαν
        καὶ τὴν γῆς κληρονομίαν
        καὶ τὰς ἐκεῖ δωρεάς;

89 πόσου ἀνετιμήσω τοὺς πάσχοντας
        οὓς αὐτὸς παρὼν ἐθεράπευσεν;   650
        τίμησαί μοι τὴν ξηρὰν χεῖρα

628 line omitted   632 ἠργυρίσω: ἀπηργυρίσω
634 πρὸς ἐμέ: πρός με   636 πλασθῆναι: καθοδηγηθῆναι
645 καὶ ἐκ: καὶ τὴν ἐκ   646 καὶ ἐν: καὶ τὴν ἐν   647 τὴν γῆς: τὴν ἐκ γῆς

86 He it is who, coming to you,
        healed your suffering and raised your dead.[37]
    He it is whom you outraged,
    he it is whom you blasphemed,
    he it is whom you oppressed,
    he it is whom you killed,
    he it is whom you extorted,
        demanding from him two drachmas as the price of his head.

87 Ungrateful Israel, come to trial with me
        concerning your ingratitude.
    How much did you value being formed by him?
    How much did you value the finding of your fathers?
    How much did you value the descent into Egypt,
        and your refreshment there under Joseph the just?

88 How much did you value the ten plagues?
    How much did you value the pillar by night,
        and the cloud by day,
        and the crossing of the Red Sea?
    How much did you value the heavenly gift of manna,
        and the water gushing from rock,
        and the giving of the law at Horeb,
        and the allotment of the land,
            and the gifts given there?

89 How much did you value the suffering ones,
        healed by his very presence?
    Give me a price on the withered hand

---

[37]The similarities in the passage just concluded with *Apostolic Constitutions* 8.12 do not necessitate a common liturgical source, but do indicate that both are drawing on a similar tradition of narrative praise.

ἣν ἀπεκατέστησεν τῷ σώματι·
τίμησαί μοι τοὺς ἐκ γενετῆς τυφλούς
οὓς διὰ φωνῆς ἐφωταγώγησεν·
τίμησαί μοι τοὺς κειμένους νεκρούς   655
οὓς ἐκ μνημείου ἀνέστησεν ἤδη τεσσάρων ἡμερῶν.

90   ἀτίμητοι αἱ παρ᾽ αὐτοῦ σοι δωρεαί·
      σὺ δὲ ἀτίμως ἀνταπέδωκας εἰς αὐτὸν τὰς χάριτας,
      ἀχαριστίας ἀνταποδοὺς αὐτῷ
            κακὰ ἀντὶ καλῶν   660
            καὶ θλῖψιν ἀντὶ χαρᾶς
            καὶ θάνατον ἀντὶ ζωῆς·
      ὑπὲρ οὗ καὶ ἀποθανεῖν σε ἔδει.

91   Εἶτα ἐὰν μὲν ἔθνους ἁρπαγῇ βασιλεὺς ὑπὸ ἐχθρῶν,
            δι᾽ αὐτὸν πόλεμος συνίσταται,   665
            δι᾽ αὐτὸν τεῖχος ῥήγνυται,
            δι᾽ αὐτὸν πόλις ἀναρπάζεται,
            δι᾽ αὐτὸν λύτρα πέμπεται,
            δι᾽ αὐτὸν πρέσβεις ἀποστέλλονται
                  ἢ ἵνα ζῶν ἀναλημφθῇ   670
                  ἢ ἵνα νεκρὸς ταφῇ.

92   σὺ δὲ τὴν ἐναντίαν κατὰ τοῦ κυρίου σου ἤνεγκας ψῆφον·
      ὃν γὰρ τὰ ἔθνη προσεκύνουν
            καὶ ἀκρόβυστοι ἐθαύμαζον
            καὶ ἀλλόφυλοι ἐδόξαζον,   675
      ἐφ᾽ ᾧ καὶ Πιλᾶτος ἐνίψατο τὰς χεῖρας,
      σὺ τοῦτον ἀπέκτεινας ἐν τῇ μεγάλῃ ἑορτῇ.

---

656 ἤδη: γ᾽ δὴ   658 χάριτας: om.
669 ἀποστέλλονται: ἀποστέλλονται ἵνα λημφθῇ
670 ἢ ἵνα ζῶν ἀναλημφθῇ: ἢ ἵνα εἰς ζωὴν ἀποστέλλονται

which he restored to its body.
Give me a price on those blind from birth
    whom he illumined by a voice.
Give me a price on those who lay dead
    and who, four days later, were raised from the tomb.

90 His gifts to you are beyond price
    yet you held them worthless when you thanked him,
      repaying him with ungrateful acts;
        evil for good,
        affliction for joy,
        and death for life.
    On this account you had to die.

91 For if the king of a nation is seized by enemies
    a war is fought on his account,
    a wall is breached on his account,
    a city is ransacked on his account,
    ransoms are sent on his account,
    envoys are sent off on his account,
      so that he might be brought back alive,
      or buried if he is dead.

92 But you cast the vote of opposition against your Lord,
      whom the Gentiles worshipped,
        at whom the uncircumcised marveled,
        whom foreigners glorified,
      over whom even Pilate washed his hands:
    for you killed him at the great feast.

93 Τοιγαροῦν πικρά σοι ἡ τῶν ἀζύμων ἑορτὴ καθώς σοι
γέγραπται·
ἔδεσθε ἄζυμα μετὰ πικρίδων.

πικροί σοι ἧλοι οὓς ὤξυνας,   680
πικρά σοι γλῶσσα ἣν παρώξυνας,
πικροί σοι ψευδομάρτυρες οὓς ἔστησας,
πικροί σοι βρόχοι οὓς ἡτοίμασας,
πικραί σοι μάστιγες ἃς ἔπλεξας,
πικρός σοι Ἰούδας ὃν ἐμισθοδότησας,   685
πικρός σοι Ἡρώδης ᾧ ἐξηκολούθησας,
πικρός σοι Καιάφας ᾧ ἐπείσθης,
πικρά σοι χολὴ ἣν ἐσκεύασας,
πικρόν σοι ὄξος ὃ ἐγεώργησας,
πικρά σοι ἄκανθα ἣν ἤνθισας,   690
πικραί σοι χεῖρες ἃς ᾕμαξας·
ἀπέκτεινάς σου τὸν κύριον ἐν μέσῳ Ἰερουσαλήμ.

94 Ἀκούσατε πᾶσαι αἱ πατριαὶ τῶν ἐθνῶν καὶ ἴδετε·
καινὸς φόνος γέγονεν ἐν μέσῳ Ἰερουσαλήμ,
ἐν πόλει νομικῇ,   695
ἐν πόλει ἑβραϊκῇ,
ἐν πόλει προφητικῇ,
ἐν πόλει δικαίᾳ νομιζομένῃ.
καὶ τίς πεφόνευται; τίς δὲ ὁ φονεύς;
εἰπεῖν αἰδοῦμαι καὶ λέγειν ἀναγκάζομαι.   700
εἰ μὲν γὰρ νύκτωρ γεγόνει ὁ φόνος,
ἢ ἐπ᾽ ἐρημίας ἦν ἐσφαγμένος,
σιγᾶν εὔχρηστον ἦν.
νῦν δὲ ἐπὶ μέσης πλατείας καὶ ἐν μέσῳ πόλεως
μέσης ἡμέρας πάντων ὁρώντων   705
γέγονεν δικαίου ἄδικος φόνος.

690 ἤνθισας: ἤμισας   704 ἐν μέσῳ πόλεως: καὶ πόλεως
705 μέσης ἡμέρας: ἐν μέσῳ πόλεως

93   Therefore the feast of unleavened bread is bitter for you:
    as it is written, "You shall eat unleavened bread with
      bitterness."
  The nails you sharpened are bitter for you,
  the tongue you incited is bitter for you,
  the false witnesses you set up are bitter for you,
  the ropes you prepared are bitter for you,
  the whips which you wove are bitter for you,
  the Judas you hired is bitter for you,
  the Herod you followed is bitter for you,
  the Caiaphas you believed is bitter for you,
  the gall you cooked up is bitter for you,
  the vinegar you produced is bitter for you,
  the thorns which you gathered are bitter for you,
  the hands which you made bloody are bitter for you.
  You killed the Lord in the middle of Jerusalem.

94   Listen all you families of the nations and see:
  a strange murder has occurred in the middle of Jerusalem;
    in the city of the law,
    in the city of the Hebrews,
    in the city of the prophets,
    in the city reckoned righteous.
  And who has been murdered? Who is the killer?
  I am ashamed to say, and I am obliged to tell.
  For if the murder took place by night,
    and if he was slaughtered in a deserted place,
      I might have been able to keep silent.
  Now in the middle of the street,
    and in the middle of the city,
      in the middle of the day before the public gaze,
      the unjust murder of a just man has taken place.

95 καὶ οὕτως ὕψωται ἐπὶ ξύλου ὑψηλοῦ·
     καὶ τίτλος πρόσκειται τὸν πεφονευμένον σημαίνων.
     τίς οὗτος; τὸ εἰπεῖν βαρὺ καὶ τὸ μὴ εἰπεῖν φοβερώτερον.
     πλὴν ἀκούσατε τρέμοντες δι᾿ ὃν ἐτρόμαξεν ἡ γῆ.   710

96 ὁ κρεμάσας τὴν γῆν κρέμαται·
     ὁ πήξας τοὺς οὐρανοὺς πέπηκται·
     ὁ στηρίξας τὰ πάντα ἐπὶ ξύλου ἐστήρικται·
     ὁ δεσπότης ὕβρισται·
     ὁ θεὸς πεφόνευται·   715
     ὁ βασιλεὺς τοῦ Ἰσραὴλ ἀνῄρηται ὑπὸ δεξιᾶς Ἰσραηλίτιδος.

97 ὢ φόνου καινοῦ, ὢ ἀδικίας καινῆς·
     ὁ δεσπότης παρεσχημάτισται γυμνῷ τῷ σώματι,
     καὶ οὐδὲ περιβολῆς ἠξίωται ἵνα μὴ θεαθῇ.
     διὰ τοῦτο οἱ φωστῆρες ἀπεστράφησαν   720
     καὶ ἡ ἡμέρα συνεσκότασεν,
     ὅπως κρύψῃ τὸν ἐπὶ ξύλου γεγυμνωμένον,
     οὐ τὸ τοῦ κυρίου σῶμα σκοτίζων
         ἀλλὰ τοὺς τῶν ἀνθρώπων ὀφθαλμούς.

98 καὶ γὰρ τοῦ λαοῦ μὴ τρέμοντος ἐτρόμαξεν ἡ γῆ·   725
     τοῦ λαοῦ μὴ φοβηθέντος ἐφοβήθησαν οἱ οὐρανοί·
     τοῦ λαοῦ μὴ περιεσχισμένου περιεσχίσατο ὁ ἄγγελος·
     τοῦ λαοῦ μὴ κωκύσαντος ἐβρόντησεν ἐξ οὐρανοῦ κύριος
         καὶ ὕψιστος ἔδωκεν φωνήν.

99 Διὰ τοῦτο, ὢ Ἰσραήλ,   730
     ἐπὶ τοῦ κυρίου οὐκ ἐτρόμαξας,
     ‹impugnatus ab hostibus contremuisti;›
     ἐπὶ τοῦ κυρίου οὐκ ἐφοβήθης,

707 ὕψωται: ὑψοῦται   ὑψηλοῦ: om.   714 ὕβρισται: παρύβρισται
725 ἐτρόμαξεν: ἔτρεμεν   731 ἐτρόμαξας: ἐτρόμησας
732 Hall supplies this from the Latin versions, Perler omits it.

95 And so he is lifted up on a tall tree
        and a placard is attached to show who has been murdered.
      Who is it? To say is hard and not to say yet more fearful.
      Listen then, shuddering at him through whom the earth
           shook.

96 He who hung the earth is hanging.
        He who fixed the heavens in place has been fixed in place.
        He who laid the foundations of the universe has been laid
           on a tree.
      The master has been profaned.
      God has been murdered.
      The King of Israel has been destroyed by an Israelite right
           hand.

97 O mystifying murder! O mystifying injustice!
      The master is obscured by his body exposed,
        and is not held worthy of a veil to shield him from view.
        For this reason the great lights turned away,
        and the day was turned to darkness;
      to hide the one denuded on the tree,
        obscuring not the body of the Lord but human eyes.

98 For when the people did not tremble, the earth shook.
        When the people did not fear, the heavens were afraid.
        When the people did not rend their garments, the angel
           rent his own.
        When the people did not lament, the Lord thundered from
           heaven,
      and the most high gave voice.

99 Therefore, Israel,
        you did not shudder at the presence of the Lord;
           so you have trembled, embattled by foes.
      You did not fear the Lord,

⟨. . . . . .⟩
ἐπὶ τοῦ κυρίου οὐκ ἐκώκυσας,   735
ἐπὶ τῶν πρωτοτόκων σου ἐκώκυσας·
κρεμαμένου τοῦ κυρίου οὐ περιεσχίσω,
ἐπὶ τῶν πεφονευμένων σου περιεσχίσω·
ἐγκατέλιπες τὸν κύριον,
οὐχ εὑρέθης ὑπ' αὐτοῦ·   740
οὐκ ἐδέξω τὸν κύριον,
οὐκ ἠλεήθης ὑπ' αὐτοῦ·
ἠδάφισας τὸν κύριον,
ἠδαφίσθης χαμαί.
καὶ σὺ μὲν κεῖσαι νεκρός,   745
ἐκεῖνος δὲ ἀνέστη ἐκ νεκρῶν
καὶ ἀνέβη εἰς τὰ ὑψηλὰ τῶν οὐρανῶν.

100 Κύριος ἐνδυσάμενος τὸν ἄνθρωπον
καὶ παθὼν διὰ τὸν πάσχοντα
καὶ δεθεὶς διὰ τὸν κρατούμενον   750
καὶ κριθεὶς διὰ τὸν κατάδικον,
καὶ ταφεὶς διὰ τὸν τεθαμμένον

101 ἀνέστη ἐκ νεκρῶν καὶ ταύτην ἐβόησεν τὴν φωνήν·
Τίς ὁ κρινόμενος πρὸς ἐμέ; ἀντιστήτω μοι.
ἐγὼ τὸν κατάδικον ἀπέλυσα·   755
ἐγὼ τὸν νεκρὸν ἐζωογόνησα·
ἐγὼ τὸν τεθαμμένον ἀνίστημι·
τίς ὁ ἀντιλέγων μοι;

102 ἐγώ, φησὶν ὁ Χριστός,
ἐγὼ ὁ καταλύσας τὸν θάνατον   760
καὶ θριαμβεύσας τὸν ἐχθρὸν

734 Perler does not indicate a lacuna here.   736 ἐκώκυσας: ἀνεκώκυσας
737 κρεμαμένου τοῦ κυρίου: ἐπὶ τοῦ κρεμαμένου κυρίου
741–742 Perler omits these lines.   754 πρὸς ἐμέ: πρός με

‹ . . . ›
You did not lament the Lord,
  so you lamented your firstborn.
When the Lord was hung up you did not rend your clothing,
  so you tore them over the fallen.
You disowned the Lord,
  and so are not owned by him.
You did not receive the Lord,
  so you were not pitied by him.
You smashed the Lord to the ground,
  you were razed to the ground.
And you lie dead
  while he rose from the dead,
    and is raised to the heights of heaven.

100 The Lord clothed himself with humanity,
      and with suffering on behalf of the suffering one,
      and bound on behalf of the one constrained,
      and judged on behalf of the one convicted,
      and buried on behalf of the one entombed,
      he rose from the dead and cried out aloud:

101 "Who takes issue with me? Let him stand before me.
      I set free the condemned.
      I gave life to the dead.
      I raise up the entombed.
      Who will contradict me?"

102 "It is I," says the Christ,
      "I am he who destroys death,
        and triumphs over the enemy,

καὶ καταπατήσας τὸν ἅδην
καὶ δήσας τὸν ἰσχυρὸν
καὶ ἀφαρπάσας τὸν ἄνθρωπον εἰς τὰ ὑψηλὰ τῶν οὐρανῶν·
ἐγώ, φησὶν, ὁ Χριστός.   765

103 τοίνυν δεῦτε πᾶσαι αἱ πατριαὶ τῶν ἀνθρώπων
αἱ ἐν ἁμαρτίαις πεφυραμέναι
καὶ λάβετε ἄφεσιν ἁμαρτημάτων.
ἐγὼ γάρ εἰμι ὑμῶν ἡ ἄφεσις,
ἐγὼ τὸ πάσχα τῆς σωτηρίας,   770
ἐγὼ ὁ ἀμνὸς ὁ ὑπὲρ ὑμῶν σφαγείς·
ἐγὼ τὸ λύτρον ὑμῶν,
ἐγὼ ἡ ζωὴ ὑμῶν,
ἐγὼ τὸ φῶς ὑμῶν,
ἐγὼ ἡ σωτηρία ὑμῶν,   775
ἐγὼ ἡ ἀνάστασις ὑμῶν,
ἐγὼ ὁ βασιλεὺς ὑμῶν·
ἐγὼ ὑμᾶς ἀναστήσω διὰ τῆς ἐμῆς δεξιᾶς·
ἐγω ὑμᾶς ανάγω εἰς τὰ ὑψηλὰ τῶν οὐρανῶν·
ἐγὼ ὑμῖν δείξω τὸν ἀπ' αἰώνων πατέρα.   780

104 Οὗτός ἐστιν ὁ ποιήσας τὸν οὐρανὸν καὶ τὴν γῆν
καὶ πλάσας ἐν ἀρχῇ τὸν ἄνθρωπον,
ὁ διὰ νόμου καὶ προφητῶν κηρυσσόμενος,
ὁ ἐπὶ παρθένῳ σαρκωθείς,
ὁ ἐπὶ ξύλῳ κρεμασθείς,   785
ὁ εἰς γῆν ταφείς,
ὁ ἐκ νεκρῶν ἀνασταθείς,

776 Perler places this line before line 774.
778 Perler places this line after line 780.

and crushes Hades,
and binds the strong man,
and bears humanity off to the heavenly heights."
"It is I," says the Christ.

103 "So come all families of people,
adulterated with sin,[38]
and receive forgiveness of sins.
For I am your freedom.
I am the Passover of salvation,
I am the lamb slaughtered for you,
I am your ransom,
I am your life,
I am your light,
I am your salvation,
I am your resurrection,
I am your King.
I shall raise you up by my right hand,
I will lead you to the heights of heaven,
there shall I show you the everlasting Father."[39]

104 He it is who made the heaven and the earth,
and formed humanity in the beginning,
who was proclaimed through the law and the prophets,
who took flesh from a virgin,
who was hung on a tree,
who was buried in earth,
who was raised from the dead,

---

[38]The word here translated "adulterated" (*pephuromenai*) has oblique reference to the leaven removed from dwellings at Passover.

[39]In this rhetorical climax we may see Melito functioning as a prophet by speaking the words of the present and risen Christ, speaking to his people in the assembly, present in his spirit as through the sacramental actions of the Pascha. The similarities with the "I am" sayings of the fourth Gospel are striking, and are not fortuitous, for they derive from a common practice of prophecy through the possession of the prophet by the spirit of Christ.

καὶ ἀνελθὼν εἰς τὰ ὑψηλὰ τῶν οὐρανῶν,
ὁ καθήμενος ἐν δεξιᾷ τοῦ πατρός,
ὁ ἔχων ἐξουσίαν πάντα σώζειν,   790
δι' οὗ ἐποίησεν ὁ πατὴρ τὰ ἀπ' ἀρχῆς μέχρι αἰώνων.

105 οὗτός ἐστιν τὸ ᾱ καὶ τὸ ῶ·
   οὗτός ἐστιν ἀρχὴ καὶ τέλος,
   ἀρχὴ ἀνεκδιήγητος καὶ τέλος ἀκατάλημπτον·
   οὗτός ἐστιν ὁ Χριστός·   795
   οὗτός ἐστιν ὁ βασιλεύς·
   οὗτός ἐστιν Ἰησοῦς·
   οὗτος <ὁ> στρατηγός·
   οὗτος ὁ κύριος·
   οὗτος ὁ ἀναστὰς ἐκ νεκρῶν·   800
   οὗτος ὁ καθήμενος ἐν δεξιᾷ τοῦ πατρός·
   φορεῖ τὸν πατέρα καὶ ὑπὸ τοῦ πατρὸς φορεῖται·
   ᾧ ἡ δόξα καὶ τὸ κράτος εἰς τοὺς αἰῶνας. ἀμήν.

Μελίτωνος Περὶ πάσχα

---

790 πάντα σώζειν: πάντα κρῖναι καὶ σώζειν

and ascended to the heights of heaven,
who sits at the right hand of the Father,
who has the power to save all things,
through whom the Father acted from the beginning and
for ever.

105 This is the alpha and omega,
this is the beginning and the end,
the ineffable beginning and the incomprehensible end.
This is the Christ,
this is the King,
this is Jesus,
this is the commander,
this is the Lord,
this is he who rose from the dead,
this is he who sits at the right hand of the Father,
he bears the Father and is borne by him.
To him be the glory and the might for ever.
Amen.

The Fragments and Other Material

Here may be found a selection of fragments from Melito's work, some testimonies to Melito and a brief selection of other material relevant to Quartodeciman practice. Not all fragments are included, for a full selection may be found in Hall. Those fragments of Melito which are certainly pseudonymous are excluded. In addition, there is a homily preserved in Coptic under the name of Athanasius, of which another version, attributed to Alexander of Alexandria, is extant in Syriac, which may well be the work of Melito, in whole or in substantial part. Further fragments are extant in Syriac, with some in Greek and a substantial amount in Georgian. This work would seem to be that *On Soul and Body* mentioned by Eusebius *Ecclesiastical History* 4.26 (see testimony "a" below). This has been excluded from the present work on grounds of size.

The numbering of the fragments here follows that of S. G. Hall, *Melito of Sardis: On Pascha and Fragments* (Oxford: Clarendon, 1979).

a) Fragment 1
(from Eusebius, *Ecclesiastical History* 4.26)

In his book to the Emperor [Marcus Aurelius] he reports that such things were happening against us in his time:

> Now the race of the God-fearing is persecuted, which is something which has never before taken place, afflicted by new decrees in Asia. For the shameless cheats and those who love the goods of others are, on this pretext, robbing openly by night

and by day, seizing the goods of those who have done nothing
wrong.

Later on he says:

And if you have commanded that this be done, let it be done
aright. For a just king would never desire that wrong be done,
and we would count it sweetness to carry off the prize of such
a death. This request alone we bring to you: that you should
first become personally acquainted with those who cause such
discord, and then consider well whether they are deserving of
death and punishment, or of prosperity and peace. If this deci-
sion and the new decree, a decree unworthy to be used against
hostile barbarians, have not come from you, then much more
do we beg of you that you should not permit us to endure state-
sponsored crime.

Then he goes on saying:

For our philosophy first flourished among the barbarians,
blossoming out among your peoples during the illustrious
reign of your ancestor Augustus, and became, especially for
your empire, a good and fortunate thing. For from then on
the strength of Rome has grown to be great and glorious. To
this you have become a much-desired successor and with your
son shall continue to be so, guarding the philosophy of the
empire, nursed and originating with Augustus. Your ancestors
respected it alongside other cults. That nothing discreditable
has befallen the empire since the reign of Augustus, when the
empire began so auspiciously, and flourished along with our
thinking is the best proof of the goodness we intend. But on
the contrary, everything has been glorious and splendid, as we
all pray that it should. Only Nero and Domitian, persuaded by
certain malicious people, were willing to put our activity under
attack. It is from them, and through unreasoning custom, that
false information about us has arisen like a flood. Your devout

ancestors corrected their ignorance, frequently, and in many writings, reprehending those who dared use force against these people. Among them your grandfather, Hadrian, wrote explicitly to Fundanus the proconsular governor of Asia, among many others. Your father, while you were governing alongside him, wrote to the city-governments that no force should be used against us. Among them he wrote to the Larissians and to the Thessalonians and to the Athenians, as to all the Greeks. On your part, since you hold the same opinion concerning these matters, and are greater in your philosophy and philanthropy, we are sure that you will do all that we ask of you.

Comment

The precise context of the new decrees is not known. In this *Apology* (to Marcus Aurelius), Melito is in accordance with the advice laid down by Menander for an address of this kind, in dwelling on the history of the imperial family and in pledging loyalty to the emperor and to his succession.[1] This is further evidence of Melito's rhetorical education.

b) Fragment 2
(from the *Paschal Chronicle* [PG 92.632A])[2]

Melito, bishop of the Sardians, says, after much which is brought forth by the aforementioned Justin: "We are not servants of stones without sense, but are worshippers of the only God who was before anything else, and above anything else, and of his Christ, who is Word of God before the ages." And so on.

---

[1]Robert M. Grant, "Five Apologists and Marcus Aurelius," *Vigiliae Christianae* 42 (1988): 1–17, at 6–7.

[2]On the authenticity of this fragment see Hall, *Melito*, xxx. For discussion see the notes on pp. 64–5.

c) Fragment 3
(from Eusebius, *Ecclesiastical History* 4.26)

In the *Extracts* which he wrote, the same author in his preface begins by listing the recognized books of the old covenant. These we must also give here. He writes as follows:

> Melito, to his brother Onesimus, greetings.
>
> Since you have often asked, in view of your great zeal for the word, that I should make for you extracts from the law and the prophets concerning the Savior and the whole of our faith, and have further desired to learn the truth about the ancient books, especially with regard to their number and the manner in which they are arranged, I have been keen to do such a thing, knowing your devotion to the faith and love of learning concerning the word and especially given that, as you strive for eternal salvation, you examine these matters more than any others which pertain to God. And so, going to the east, where these matters were spoken and performed, I learned there the books of the old covenant with accuracy. Now I send you my treatise.
>
> These are their names. There are five books of Moses: Genesis, Exodus, Numbers, Leviticus, Deuteronomy. Joshua the son of Nave, Judges, Ruth, four books of Kingdoms, two books of Omissions, the Psalms of David, the Proverbs and the Wisdom of Solomon, Ecclesiastes, the Song of Songs, Job, and among the prophets Isaiah and Jeremiah. There are twelve prophets in one book, and Daniel, Ezekiel and Esdras. From these I have made my extracts, which are divided into six books.

Comment

This fragment is highly significant as the first Christian Old Testament canon. It is also of interest that Melito travelled to Palestine, and his list is thus an indication that this is the Old Testament canon known by Palestinian Christians, and perhaps Jews. The statement that "these matters were spoken and performed" is interesting since this is a standard definition of a *chreia*, or short aphoristic story, which was a standard element in rhetorical education. The use of this summary of Scripture would imply that Melito understood his extracts from Scripture as a collection of *chreiai*. See also Fragment 15 below, which some suspect to have derived from the *Extracts*.

D) FRAGMENT 4
(from Eusebius, *Ecclesiastical History* 4.26)

In his work "Concerning the Pascha" he indicates the time at which he drew it up at the beginning, stating thus:

> When Servillius Paulus was proconsul of Asia, and Sagaris was martyred at a fitting time, there was a great dispute in Laodicea concerning the Pascha, which fell most fittingly in those days. And these things were written:
>
>> Clement the Alexandrian records this matter in his own work concerning the Pascha which he says he composed because of Melito's writing

Comment

For a full discussion of this fragment see the introduction; there it is argued that this is not by Melito at all, but is a scribe's introductory note to Melito's work which Eusebius has copied in error.

E) FRAGMENT 5
(from Origen *Comments on the Psalms* [PG 12.1120A])

Thus Melito in Asia says that he is a type of the devil, rebelling against the Kingdom of Christ; he did not give a full treatment of the topic, but simply mentions this.

Comment

The subject is Absalom, and the subject of comment is Psalm 3, the heading of which states that the Psalm was composed when David was fleeing Absalom. Whereas this may be from the work *On the Devil and the Apocalypse*, the fact that, according to Origen, Melito simply mentions this in passing is an indication that this statement is made in the context of a typological treatment of the suffering of Christ.

f) Fragment 7
(Anastasius of Sinai *The Guide* 12 [PG 89.197A])

Of Melito, the bishop of Sardis, from his book on the passion: God has been murdered by an Israelite right hand.

Comment

This fragment, a slight misquotation of *On Pascha* 95, is included since it was the basis on which the original identification of the papyrus was made by Bonner, the first editor of the work.

g) Fragment 8b
(J. B. Pitra, *Analecta Sacra* II 3–5)

By Melito of Sardis: On Baptism

What kind of gold or silver or bronze or iron is not burned red hot and then dipped in water, either to be brightened in color or so that it can be tempered through its dipping? Indeed, the whole earth is washed with rains and rivers, and farms well after it is bathed. In the same way the land of Egypt is washed by a river in swell, and the cornfield grows and the ear is full, and it yields one hundredfold through the goodly bath. Even the air itself is washed by the rain-drops falling. The mother of rains, the multicolored rainbow, itself bathes, when she lures rivers down gullies with watery breath.

If you wish to see the heavenly bodies being dipped go off now to the ocean, and there I shall show you a strange sight. The spread-out sea and the boundless foam and the infinite deep and the measureless ocean and the pure water: the bath-chamber of the sun, the place where the stars are brightened, and the moon's pool. Learn then faithfully from me how they bathe symbolically.

For the sun, when it has run its daily course with its fiery chariot, having in the course of its run become fiery and burning like a lamp, having burned up in the middle of its circular run then, lest he come close by and ignite the earth as though with ten lightning shafts, dips in the ocean. In the same way a sphere of bronze, full of interior fire, and shedding much light, is dipped in cold water with a loud noise and leaves off burning. But the fire within is not extinguished but returns once more when it is roused. In the same way then the sun, having flamed like lightning, is bathed in cold water but does not cease to burn entirely, for its fire is unsleeping. When he has washed in this symbolic bath he rejoices greatly, having water for food. He is one and the same sun, although he appears to people as new; he has been tempered in the deep and purified in a bath. He has driven the darkness of night away and begets a bright day. Along his course operate the movement of the stars and the appearance of the moon. For they bathe in the bath-chamber of the sun as faithful disciples. For the stars and the moon together follow the trail of the sun, permeated by his pure brilliance.

If the sun, together with the stars and the moon, is bathed in the ocean, why should Christ not bathe in the Jordan, the King of the heavens and the ruler of creation, the sun of uprising who appeared to mortals in Hades and on earth alike, and who rose alone as a sun out of heaven?

Comment

Remarkable parallels between this fragment on baptism and stoic exegesis of Homer have been noted.[3] The first section, concerning

[3]By Robert M. Grant, "Melito of Sardis on Baptism," *Vigiliae Christianae* 4 (1950): 33–6.

the uses of water, contains images generally found in stoic treatments of the doctrine of providence. Stoics had a particular interest in the interpretation of poetry, and so the technical background to Melito's study here is almost certainly Homeric exegesis. This is exactly what one would expect from the author of *On Pascha*, where there is a section which engages with the question of exegetical method in a stoic manner. As part of his rhetorical training Melito would have learnt the schools of Homeric interpretation. The authenticity of this fragment has been doubted, but there are grounds for seeing it as authentic, quite apart from the fact that the author of this fragment shared an educational background with Melito. The main reason for suggesting inauthenticity is stylistic but the difference in style between this fragment (reminiscent in many ways of a school exercise) and *On Pascha* may be accounted for by recognizing the difference in genre. *On Pascha* is liturgical; this fragment is controversial. Compare, also, the inscription SB 1.4127 (most easily accessible in A.D. Nock, "A vision of Mandulis Aion," *Harvard Theological Review* 27 (1934): 53–104) for the idea of the sun taking a purificatory bath in the ocean at setting.

h) FRAGMENTS 9–11
(from a catena published by J. B. Pitra, *Spicilegium Solesmense*, II lxiii s)

Fragment 9

Of blessed Melito of Sardis.

> As a ram he was bound,
> he says concerning our Lord Jesus Christ,
>> and as a lamb he was shorn,
>> and as a sheep he was led to slaughter,
>> and as a lamb he was crucified.
> And he bore the wood on his shoulders,

going up to slaughter like Isaac at the hand of his father.
But Christ suffered.
Isaac did not suffer,
   for he was a type of the passion of Christ which was to
      come.
Yet even the type caused fear and astonishment to come upon
      people.
For it was a strange mystery to behold:
   the son led up a mountain by his father, for slaughter,
   whose feet he bound onto the wood of the offering,
   preparing with haste for the slaughter to come.

Isaac was silent whilst bound like a ram,
   not opening his mouth nor uttering a word.
He did not fear the knife,
   nor did he panic at the fire,
   nor did he grieve at his suffering.
The type of the Lord he bore bravely.
In the midst was Isaac offered,
   like a ram bound at his feet.
     And Abraham was present and held the knife unsheathed,
       not ashamed to put his son to death.

Fragment 10

Of Melito of Sardis

   On behalf of Isaac, the righteous one, there appeared a ram for
      slaughter
    so that Isaac could be set free from his bonds.
   The ram was slaughtered and ransomed Isaac:
   in the same way the Lord was slaughtered and saved us,
     and freed us from our bonds,
     and ransomed us through his sacrifice.

Fragment 11

A little later:

> For the Lord was a lamb like the ram which Abraham saw
> caught in a Sabek tree.
> But the tree displayed the cross,
> and that place showed forth Jerusalem,
> and the lamb showed forth the Lord, tied up for slaughter.

Comment

The chief interest in these fragments, all of which come from the same collection of testimonies, is Melito's use of traditions deriving from Judaism concerning the redemptive effect of the sacrifice of Isaac and his concern to counter them. Melito refers to this theme in *On Pascha* 59 and 69, where Isaac is a type of Jesus. We may perhaps see some hint of Isaac typology in John's Gospel, in which Jesus, like Isaac, carries the wood (the cross) for his own sacrifice, and we should also observe that there are a number of references to Isaac's sacrifice in *The Martyrdom of Polycarp*. Melito is concerned to stress that Jesus is greater than Isaac in that he is actually sacrificed and dies.[4]

I) FRAGMENT 14
(from a Christological collection published by Ignaz Rucker,
Florilegium Edessenum anonymum [Munich: Bayerische Akademie
der Wissenchaften, 1933], 14–16)

Of the same, from his speech concerning the cross:

> On account of these matters he came to us,
> on account of these matters he, who was disembodied, formed
> himself a body of our substance.

[4]For further discussion see Robert L. Wilken, "Melito, the Jewish Community at Sardis and the Sacrifice of Isaac," *Theological Studies* 37 (1976): 53–69.

He appeared as a sheep while remaining a shepherd,
he was thought to be a slave, while not denying his sonship,
he was born of Mary, while wearing the garment of his Father,
walking on earth whilst filling the heavens,
appearing as a child, whilst not falsifying the eternity of his
     nature,
clothed in flesh whilst not constraining the simplicity of his
     divinity.
Believed to be poor, but not deprived of his wealth,
requiring nourishment, insofar as he was a needy human,
   not ceasing to nourish the world, as he was God.
Putting on the likeness of a slave while not altering his likeness
     to the Father.
In his unchangeable nature he was all things.
He stood before Pilate and is seated with the Father,
he was nailed on the tree and comprehended all things.

Comment

It is not certain that the entirety of this fragment is the work of
Melito; as Nautin points out, the statements regarding the unalter-
ability of Christ's divine nature and the likeness to the Father betray
the vocabulary and concerns of the fourth century Arian controversy,[5] but the contrast between the glory of God and the abasement
of the incarnate Christ is found particularly in the work *On Soul and
Body*. It is thus possible that an authentic statement of Melito has
been altered and expanded.

[5]Pierre Nautin, *Le dossier d'Hippolyte et de Méliton dans les florilèges dogmatiques
et chez les historiens modernes* (Paris: Cerf, 1953), 73.

j) Fragment 15
(from a Christological collection published by Rucker, *Florilegium Edessenum anonymum*, 55–60)[6]

From Melito the bishop, on faith:

I have gathered from the law and the prophets what is announced regarding Our Lord Jesus Christ in order to demonstrate to you, beloved, that he is perfect intellect, the word of God who was begotten before the morning star.[7] He, with the Father, is the Creator, he is the one who formed humanity, he is all in all.[8]

He was a patriarch among the patriarchs,
he was a law among the laws,
   a chief-priest among the priests,
   a leader among the kings,
   a prophet among the prophets,

---

[6]The textual history of this fragment is of exceptional complexity. The translation is that of the Syriac version from the Edessene florilegium, which attributes it to Melito. Another version is attributed to Irenaeus, and is found in an Armenian translation of a florilegium of Timothy Aelurus and (in abbreviated form) in Ethiopic and Arabic translations of a Coptic version. The introductory lines are also quoted by Severus of Antioch, preserved in Syriac. The easiest way to follow this is through the discussion of Hermann Jordan, *Armenische Irenaeusfragmente mit deutscher Übersetzung nach Dr W. Lüdtke* (TU 36.3; Leipzig: Hinrich, 1913), 56–60, where variations between the versions are noted. Jordan prints the Arabic and Ethiopic versions as well as the Armenian. Finally there is a clear debt to this work in a Greek prayer attributed to John Chrysostom, published by Marcel Richard, "Témoins grecs des fragments XIII et XV de Méliton de Sardes," *Le Muséon* 85 (1972): 309–36, at 318–21, and a Greek version of the introductory paragraph, attributed to Irenaeus and in the Irenaean form, in a Florilegium also edited by Marcel Richard, "Le florilège du Cod. Vatopédi 236 sur le corruptible et l'incorruptible," *Le Muséon* 86 (1973): 249–73, here at 265. These are noted in the footnotes below.

[7]Ps 110 (109).3.

[8]Cf. the Irenaean version: "The law and the prophets proclaimed Christ, born of a virgin and suffering on the tree, appearing from the dead and gone up to the heaven, exalted by the Father and king for ever. He is the perfect intellect . . . " Apart from its appearance in the versions attributed to Irenaeus this opening is reflected in the version found in Codex Vatopedi 236 (see footnote 6 above).

among the angels an archangel,
a Word in the voice,
a spirit among spirits,[9]
a Son in the Father,
a god in God,
king for ever and ever.
For he it was who was Noah's steersman,
he was Abraham's guide,
he was bound with Isaac,
he was in exile with Jacob,
he was sold with Joseph,
he was a leader with Moses,[10]
he divided the inheritance with Joshua, son of Nun.
By David and the prophets he announced his sufferings.
He was enfleshed of a virgin,
he was born at Bethlehem,
he was wrapped in bands in a manger,
he was known by shepherds,
he was praised by angels,
he was adored by magi,
he was foretold by John,[11]
he gathered the apostles,
he proclaimed the Kingdom,
he healed the lame,[12]
he enlightened the blind,
he raised the dead,

---

[9]For "a word in the voice, a spirit among spirits" the Irenaean version has "a man amidst humanity."

[10]The Irenaean version adds: "he gave the people the law." This is reflected in the prayer of Chrysostom.

[11]The Irenaean version adds: "and was baptized in the Jordan, he was tempted in the desert and found to be the Lord." Reference to the baptism, and to the temptation in the desert linked to the recognition of Christ as God is also found in the prayer of Chrysostom.

[12]The Irenaean version adds: "he purified the lepers." This is reflected in the prayer of Chrysostom.

he appeared in the temple,
he was disbelieved by the people,
he was betrayed by Judas,
he was taken by the priests,[13]
he was judged by Pilate,
he was nailed up in the flesh,
he was hanged on a tree,
he was buried in the earth,
he rose up from the realm of the dead,
he appeared to the apostles,
he was lifted to the heavens,
he sits to the right of the Father.
He it is who is rest for the dying,
redeemer of the lost,
light of those in darkness,
and Savior of those who are falling,
guide of those who are wandering,
place of refuge for those in despair,[14]
bridegroom of the church,
charioteer of the cherubim,
leader of the hosts of angels,
God from God,
Son from the Father,
Jesus Christ, King for eternity.
Amen.

Comment

Although this fragment is widely suggested to be from Melito's *Extracts*, on the basis of the opening paragraph, the Irenaean version, which is otherwise more complete, tends to suggest that this opening may not be original and may be the result of subsequent

[13]The Irenaean version adds: "he was led before Herod". This is reflected in the prayer of Chrysostom.

[14]The Irenaean version adds here "shepherd of the redeemed." The prayer of Chrysostom has "good shepherd of the sheep."

redaction. Such is the complexity of the textual tradition that we can only uphold the attribution on the grounds of similarity with *Peri Pascha* and some common turns of phrase in the work *On Soul and Body.* However, even if this is not from the *Extracts* we may observe Melito's conviction, similarly evinced in *On Pascha,* that Christ was active through the events of the old covenant, and see that this might likewise be the motivating factor behind his production of the *Extracts.*

к) FRAGMENT 16B
(in Marcel Richard, "Témoins grecs des fragments XIII et XV de Méliton de Sardes," *Le Muséon* 85 (1972): 309–36, at 324)

From Melito, Bishop of Sardis, in the discourse regarding the Lord's day.

> "For who knows the mind of the Lord, or who was his
>   counsellor?"[15] except the Word, who was enfleshed in the
>   virgin, and buried in earth,
>   and raised from the dead,
> who was exalted to the heavens and glorified in the Father.

L) FRAGMENT 17
(Bodmer Papyrus XII)

You saints sing hymns to the father,
you maidens sing to the mother.
We hymn them, we saints lift them high.
You have been exalted to be brides and bridegrooms,
for you have found your bridegroom Christ.
Drink for wine, brides and bridegrooms. . . .

---

[15] Is 40.13; Rom 11.34.

Comment

This fragment is found in Bodmer Papyrus XII, following on from *On Pascha*.[16] It is not actually attributed to Melito, but Perler suggests that it is part of the Quartodeciman liturgy, and that it is the beginning of the second book mentioned by Eusebius.[17] But although, as a hymn, this is a liturgical fragment, this does not mean it is necessarily the work of Melito, nor is there any certainty whether this is part of the other book, assuming that such a book ever existed. Perler suggested that the liturgy was baptismal and followed on from the invitation to forgiveness at the end of *On Pascha*. But not only is there no definite reference to baptism in *On Pascha*, the function of *On Pascha* as a liturgy of commemoration rather precludes a further baptismal rite. The papyrus is itself a collection of miscellaneous material from distinct hands; thus the connection between *Peri Pascha* and this fragment is even more tenuous. However, it has also been suggested that the codex is a collection of materials which had already been collected, and that earlier in the chain of transmission a scribe saw a link between *Peri Pascha* and the hymnic fragment, copying them together prior to their inclusion into the existing codex.[18] Thus, although Perler's suggestion is to be rejected, it is not impossible that a scribe saw the appropriateness of appending a hymnic fragment to *Peri Pascha* on the basis of a recognition of a hymnic element in the paschal vigil.[19]

[16]See the introduction p. 20.

[17]Othmar Perler, *Ein Hymnus zur Ostervigil von Meliton? (Papyrus Bodmer 12)*, Paradosis 15 (Freiburg, Schweiz: Universitätsverlag, 1960).

[18]Tommy Wassermann, "Papyrus 72 and the *Bodmer Miscellaneous Codex*," *New Testament Studies* 51 (2005): 137–54, at 146.

[19]Cf., however, Thomas Scott Caulley, "A Fragment of an Early Christian Hymn (Papyrus Bodmer 12): Some Observations," *Zeitschrift für Antikes Christentum/Journal of Ancient Christianity* 13 (2009): 403–14, who rejects any connection outright.

Testimonies to Melito
from later authors

A) FROM EUSEBIUS
Ecclesiastical History 4.26

At this time both Melito, the bishop of the community in Sardis, and Apollinarius of that in Hierapolis were flourishing and prominent. Each individually addressed an apology in these times to the emperor of Rome mentioned above, in defense of the faith. Treatises have come down by these people to our knowledge: of Melito, two books on the Pascha, *On Conduct and the Prophets*, that *Concerning the Church*, and the work *Concerning the Lord's Day*. Then there is that *Concerning Human Faith*, and that *On the Creation* and that *On the Obedience of Faith and on Sense*, and additionally that *Concerning the Soul and the Body and their Union*, and that *On Baptism* and that *On the Truth* and *On the Foundation and the Birth of Christ*. And his work *On Prophecy*, and that *Concerning Hospitality* and *The Key*. And that *Concerning the Devil and the Apocalypse of John*, and that *On the Embodiment of God* and last of all the short book to Antoninus.

Comment

The remainder of Eusebius' testimony is made up of the three extracts from Melito's work found above numbered as 1, 3 and 4 (of which 4 is not actually by Melito!). The text of Eusebius' list here is impossibly corrupt, and the division of the words into titles, and in some cases the words themselves, is little more than intelligent guesswork. The probability is that Eusebius had done little more than consult a library catalogue, or perhaps more than one catalogue, and for this reason we should not be overmuch exercised by the reference to "two books on the Pascha."[1]

b) From Jerome
On Famous Men 24

Melito the Asian, the bishop of Sardis, gave a book to the Emperor Marcus Antoninus Verus, who was a disciple of the orator Fronto, on behalf of the Christian faith. He wrote other books, and these are some which we catalogue here: Two books *On the Pascha*, one book *On the Life of Prophets*, one book *On the Church*, one book *On the Lord's Day*, one book *On the Senses*, one book *Concerning Faith*, one book *On Creation*, one book *On the Soul and the Body*, one book *Concerning Baptism*, one book *On the Truth*, one book *On the Generation of Christ*, one book *Concerning his Prophecy*, one book *On Hospitality* and another book which is called *The Key*. One book *On the Devil*, one book *On the Apocalypse of John*, one book *On the Embodiment of God* and six books of *Extracts*. In the seven books that he wrote against the church on behalf of Montanus, Tertullian complains at his elegant and declamatory genius, and adds that he is considered by some of us to be a prophet.

Comment

The list of works is clearly based on that of Eusebius and has no independent value. The snippet on Tertullian's cavil however is interesting. For Tertullian to complain at another's declamatory style is extraordinary, though the substance of his report of Melito's style is borne out in *On Pascha*. The report of Melito's prophecy bears out the reading of the final sections of *On Pascha* as ecstatic prophecy spoken in the name of Christ. The interesting question

[1]There is a thorough discussion of this list, including reference to the textual problems, in Hall, *Melito of Sardis on Pascha*, xiii–xvii.

is, who considered Melito a prophet? Although Jerome would be indicating that the catholic side (of the catholic-Montanist debate) recognized Melito's prophecy, the use of "us" in Tertullian usually indicates that he is referring to the pro-Montanist sub-group within the church at Carthage, and it is possible that Jerome has been careless in his citation, and that Tertullian, who does not reckon Melito a prophet, is angered at his fellow-Montanist sympathizers who nonetheless recognize Melito's prophecy. Certainly there is every indication here that Melito was considered a prophet by his contemporaries, and that this provides grounds for us to understand his work in this light.

Selections from other authors concerning Quartodeciman practice

A) APOLLINARIUS
(from the *Paschal Chronicle* [PG 92.80–81])

Apollinarius, the most holy bishop of Hierapolis in Asia, who was roughly contemporary with the apostles, taught similarly in his treatise on the Pascha, saying as follows:

> Now there are some who through ignorance love to quarrel about these matters: but what they maintain in this affair is forgivable. For ignorance does not respond well to accusations, but may be amenable to teaching. And they say that on the fourteenth day the Lord ate the sheep with the disciples, and that on the great day of unleavened bread he suffered, and they say that Matthew speaks thus, according to their interpretation. But their thinking is not in accordance with the law, and the Gospels conspire to refute them.

In the same work the same writer speaks thus:

> The fourteenth is the true Pascha of the Lord,
> the great sacrifice,
> the son of God standing in place of the lamb.
> The one being bound is the one who bound the strong
>   man,
> and the one being judged is the judge of the living and the
>   dead.

And the one who is betrayed into the hands of sinners to
    be crucified is raised above the horns of the unicorn.
And the one whose holy side was pierced
poured forth from his side the two purifications:
water and blood,
word and spirit.
He is buried on the day of Pascha,
and a stone is put over his tomb.

Comment

The second of these two fragments is a classic statement of Quartodeciman theology; there is no doubt that Apollinarius was a Quartodeciman, despite some avowals to the contrary. He also wrote against Montanism and is clearly a rough contemporary of Melito. The dispute which is mentioned here is a matter of much debate; I have argued elsewhere that there was some debate among Quartodecimans about the time of the paschal celebration (though there was agreement on the date). Some kept it in the evening, and justified their practice with reference to synoptic accounts of Jesus eating the Passover with his disciples, whereas others (Apollinarius and, probably, Melito among them) kept it at midnight and justified their practice with reference to John. Both justifications are secondary. Those who kept Pascha in the evening understood it to be a repetition of the Last Supper, whereas those who kept at night reckoned it a commemoration of the passion and resurrection, as is implied by Melito's work.[1]

---

[1] For full bibliography and discussion see Alistair Stewart-Sykes, *The Lamb's High Feast* (Leiden: Brill, 1998), 147–60, but note the caveat in the footnote below.

B) HIPPOLYTUS
(from the *Paschal Chronicle* [PG 92.80–81])

Hippolytus now, a martyr of sanctity, who was the Bishop of Porto near Rome, writes in this way in his anthology against all the heresies:

> I see now what the cause of the disquiet is. For somebody might say "Christ kept the Pascha and then, during the day, he died. It is necessary for me to do what the Lord did, just as he did it." They are in error in not realizing that Christ suffered (*epaschen*) at this hour, and did not eat (*ephagen*) the Pascha according to the law. Thus he was himself the Pascha which was announced in advance, and which was fulfilled on the appointed day.

(from the *Refutation of all the heresies* 8.18)

> There are others, fractious by nature, individualistic in their understanding, pugnacious over the point, who maintain that it is necessary to keep the Pascha on the fourteenth of the first month in accordance with the provision of the law, on whatever day it might fall. They have regard only to that which is written in the law that whosoever does not keep it as it is commanded is accursed. They do not notice that the law was laid down for the Jews, who in time would destroy the true Passover, which has come to the Gentiles and is discerned by faith, and not by observation of the letter. By keeping to this one commandment they do not notice what was said by the apostle, namely, "I bear witness to everyone who is circumcised that they are obliged to keep the entirety of the law." In other things they conform to everything which has been handed down to the Church by the apostles.

Comment

Hippolytus is widely assumed to be writing in these passages against Quartodeciman practice.[2] It is however possible that he was himself of Asian or Syrian lineage, which means that he might himself be a Quartodeciman. If this could be imagined for a moment we might see that rather than writing against Quartodecimans he is defending the practice of keeping Pascha at midnight rather than in the evening at the same time as the Jewish festivity, using a similar line of argument to Apollinarius. On this understanding his opponent is a Quartodeciman who believes that the synoptic chronology and the law alike point in the direction of keeping Pascha as the fulfillment of the Last Supper; Hippolytus replies by suggesting that the true fulfillment of the Pascha is not the Last Supper but the manner in which the Lord fulfilled and completed the provisions of the law by suffering (*paschein*) rather than eating (*phagein*). The manner in which both Hippolytus and Apollinarius refer to the fractious and difficult nature of their opponents is also an indication that the dispute is not between Sunday-keepers and Quartodecimans but between Quartodecimans with different understandings of the time at which to keep the Pascha, and thus of what it means to keep the Pascha.

c) Eusebius' account of the Quartodeciman controversy at Rome at the end of the second century
(*Ecclesiastical History* 5.23–4)

23 Now there was stirred up at that time a dispute of no small moment, for all the residents of Asia, for whom this was an ancient tradition, held it necessary to keep the feast of the Pascha of the Savior on the fourteenth day of the moon, when the Jews are com-

[2]An erroneous assumption which I made myself in *The Lamb's High Feast*, 157–58. I withdraw my criticism on this point of G. Visonà, "Pasqua Quartodecimana e cronologia evangelica della passione," *Ephemerides Liturgicae* 102 (1988): 259–315.

manded to sacrifice the sheep. They held it required at all costs to put an end to their fasting on that day, regardless of what day of the week it was. This was not in accordance with the custom and manner of all the churches in the rest of the world, who, according to apostolic tradition maintained the custom which had come to them that they should not conclude the fast except on the day of the resurrection of our Savior. Synods and gatherings of bishops were convened on this matter and all with one mind drew up the Church's opinion for universal dissemination. They decreed that the mystery should not be celebrated except on the Sunday on which the Lord rose from the dead, and that on that day alone should the paschal fast be concluded. The writing which came from those who were gathered in Palestine, who were brought together under Theophilus, bishop of the community of Caesarea, and Narcissus, of the community in Jerusalem, is extant to this day. The same is true of another communication from Rome concerning the same dispute, which shows that Victor was the bishop. There is another from the bishops in Pontus, over whom Palmas, as the oldest, presided, and from the communities of Gaul which Irenaeus governed. And there is yet another from Osrhoene and the cities there. And similarly from Bacchyllus, the bishop of the church of the Corinthians, and a host of others, who expressed one and the same opinion, and gave the same judgement. And so there was one decree, as we have shown.

Comment

Victor was simply a bishop among others, in what was still a loose confederation of churches. The episcopal office in Rome grew out of the office of the presbyter whose duty it was to correspond with other churches; it is still in this capacity that Victor is corresponding with other churches in the world over a matter which concerned Rome, and it is from this that Eusebius deduces that he was the sole bishop. It would seem that Asian churches in Rome were continuing their Quartodeciman practice, and that this was an obstacle in the gradual unification of the Roman churches under a single acknowledged bishop; quite why Victor is addressing himself to communities outside of Rome over a purely internal matter is not clear, but it is possible that Asian (and other Quartodeciman) communities in Rome had appealed to their home bishops, and so Victor is attempting to set the record straight.

24 Polycrates was the leader of the bishops of Asia, who firmly maintained that they should keep the custom which had been handed down to them from ancient times. And he himself sets down the tradition as it had come down to him in the following letter that he wrote to Victor and to the church of the Romans.

> For we keep the day without interference, neither adding nor subtracting. And there are in Asia great lights who have died, and will rise again on the day of the coming of the Lord, when he comes with glory from the heavens and shall raise all the saints: Philip of the twelve apostles, who lies in Hierapolis, and two of his daughters who grew old in virginity. And there is another daughter of his who rests, having served the church in the Holy Spirit. And there is indeed John who lay on the breast of the Lord, who was a priest wearing the breastplate, and who was a martyr and a teacher.[3] He lies at Ephesus. And indeed there is Polycarp in Smyrna, both bishop and martyr, and Thraseas from Eumeneia, who lies at Smyrna. And is it necessary to speak of Sagaris, bishop and martyr, who lies at Laodicea? And there is Papirius the blessed, and Melito the eunuch, who governed all things in the Holy Spirit, and who lies at Sardis awaiting the visitation from the heavens when he shall be raised from the dead. All of these kept the fourteenth day as the Pascha in accordance with the Gospel, not deviating from the rule of faith but maintaining it. And then there is myself, Polycrates, the least of all; I have kept to the tradition of my race, some of

---

[3]For an extensive discussion of this puzzling reference see Richard Bauckham, "Papias and Polycrates on the Origin of the Fourth Gospel," *Journal of Theological Studies* 44 (1993): 24–69.

whom I have followed. For seven of my race were bishops, and I am the eighth.[4] And my race always kept the day when the people put away the leaven. I therefore, brothers, sixty-five years in the Lord and having had commerce with brothers from the whole world and having spanned the whole of holy Scripture, am not frightened by threats. For those better than I have said: we should obey God rather than people.[5]

To these remarks he adds comment concerning the many bishops who were present with him and agreed with him.

I might record the bishops who are with me, whom I invited when you desired that I should invite them. If I should write their names they would be a great multitude. They see me, the least of men, and they have approved this letter, knowing that I do not have grey hair for nothing but that I have conducted myself always in the Lord Jesus.

At this, Victor, presiding over Rome, sought to cut off straightaway the churches of all of the community of Asia from the common union, together with those which neighbored upon them, on the grounds of heterodoxy. He denounced them in letters proclaiming that the brethren there were entirely out of union. But this was not to the liking of all the overseers, and they pleaded with him to have a mind to those things which are conducive to peace and to unity with one's neighbors and to common charity. These letters are extant, criticizing Victor severely. Among them was Irenaeus, who wrote in his capacity as leader of the brethren in Gaul, in which he states that one should keep the day of the resurrection of the Lord on the Lord's day alone. Yet he takes Victor to task for cutting of entire churches on the grounds that they kept an ancient custom which had been

---

[4]See the introduction, pp. 14–15, for some discussion of what Polycrates means by his reference to his race. Although Polycrates considers himself a minor figure in comparison to his predecessors, he is clearly the acknowledged leader of the Asian bishops, though whether this results from family connections, wealth, age, or the occupation of the see held by John, cannot be said.

[5]Acts 5.29. Polycrates is quoting Peter!

handed down to them, and he gives much counsel besides, adding, in these words:

> For the controversy is not only about the day, but also concerning the very form of the fast. For there are those who hold that one should fast a single day, others two, and others more. Some count "the day" as forty continuous hours of day and night. And the great variety of observance did not come about in our day, but came from much earlier, from those who went before us, who held closely to their customary ways, perhaps in their simplicity, and so things have been done until our time. But nonetheless all of these were at peace, and we likewise live in peace with one another. Indeed, the distinction in fasting emphasizes the harmony of our faith.

To these remarks he adds the following account, which I may suitably quote, since this is its proper place:

> Among them were the elders before Soter, who presided over the church which you now lead. We mean Anicetus and Pius, Hyginus and Telesphorus and Sixtus. None of them observed, nor did any of those who were with them. And yet those who did not observe kept peace with those from the communities in which the observance was kept, and they engaged with one another. And the custom of observance was all the more difficult to those who did not observe at all. And never was anyone cast out over this affair, but those elders before you who did not observe nonetheless sent the Eucharist to those from the communities who observed. And when the blessed Polycarp was at Rome in the time of Anicetus, although there were many other matters on which they had differences, they maintained peace with one another, not wanting to fall out with one another over this matter. Anicetus was not able to persuade Polycarp not to observe, as he had with John the disciple of our Lord and the other disciples with whom he had associated, and as

he had always observed. Nor moreover did Polycarp persuade Anicetus to observe, for he said that he should be faithful to the custom of the elders before him. And although matters stood thus, nonetheless Anicetus yielded presidency of the Eucharist to Polycarp in the church, clearly out of respect for him. And they parted from one another in peace, as indeed the entire church had peace between those who observed and those who did not observe.

Comment

Although Eusebius does not understand the material with which he is dealing, since he clearly treats Victor not only as a monarch-bishop in Rome but as a bishop having authority even beyond the city, the phrases that he uses are possibly derived from ancient documents. Victor is not excommunicating Polycrates, but Asian churches within Rome, and the common union from which they are expelled is the union of churches within Rome. Irenaeus' mention of the sending of the Eucharist would seem to be a reference to the ancient Roman rite of the *fermentum*, in which churches in the city would send portions of the Eucharist to the other churches in the city as a sign of their union. It is this sign of union which is withdrawn and which, according to Irenaeus, should be sent even though there is some difference among the Roman churches. Irenaeus was himself Asian in origin, though he would seem not to be keeping Quarto-deciman practice in Gaul, and he points out that there are differences even among the Quartodecimans with regard to the length of the fast which is kept before Pascha.

The references to "observing" however in Irenaeus' letter are matters of great controversy, as the verb has no object.

An implied object might be:

a) The fast, by which Irenaeus means that some did not observe an extended fast before Pascha;

b) The feast, by which Irenaeus means that some did not observe a Pascha at all; or

c) The fourteenth day, which would imply that some at Rome observed Pascha on a Sunday, others on the fourteenth day.

All of these are historically possible (though grammatically the second suggestion is difficult and the first is easiest, especially since Irenaeus in the previous passage has used the same verb to refer to the fast). However, not observing the fast might be an implication that the feast was not observed either; the eventual compromise to which the Tiburtine tables point, that the Pascha was set on the Sunday following the fourteenth Nisan and that the fast would begin on the fourteenth, would be a reasonable compromise between those who observed no fast or annual festival and held that Sunday was the only proper day for the (weekly) commemoration of the resurrection and those who observed Pascha on the fourteenth Nisan. But this still leaves us blind to the majority Roman practice between Soter and Victor. Victor is moving the Roman church towards monepiscopacy, and therefore desires some measure of liturgical uniformity in any event, but the problem would be all the more acute should the fast fall on a Sunday and therefore displace the usual Sunday celebration. This is why Irenaeus points out that those who did not observe nonetheless sent the Eucharist to the non-observers; that is to say that although the Quartodecimans might be observing no celebration on a particular Sunday the non-Quartodeciman Roman Christians nonetheless sent them a portion of the Eucharist. Thus the solution proposed here is that on grammatical grounds we should read "fast" as the object of "observe," but that the effect of this was that those who observed no fast observed no feast either.[6]

---

[6]For a fuller discussion and bibliography see *The Lamb's High Feast*, 205.

D) FROM THE *LIFE OF POLYCARP* 1[7]

In the days of unleavened bread, Paul, coming down from Galatia, arrived in Asia, intending from there to go on to Jerusalem. He thought that to be among the faithful in Smyrna was a great relief after his immense labor in the Lord Jesus Christ. In Smyrna he visited Strataias, who had heard him in Pamphylia, and was the son of Eunike, the daughter of Lois. They are mentioned in his writing to Timothy, when he speaks of "the unfeigned faith which is in you, as it dwelt first in your grandmother Lois and in your mother Eunike" (2 Tim 1.5). From this we may deduce that Strataias was Timothy's brother. When he arrived, Paul gathered those who were faithful and spoke to them about the Pascha and the Pentecost, reminding them about the new covenant of the offering of the bread and the cup, how they should be sure always to celebrate it in the days of unleavened bread, holding fast to the new mystery of the passion and the resurrection. Here the apostle is clearly teaching us that we should not do this outside of the period of the unleavened bread, as do the heretics, and especially the Phrygians, but that we should not be obliged to keep the fourteenth day; for nowhere is the fourteenth mentioned, but he mentions the day of unleavened bread, the Pascha and the Pentecost, in keeping with the Gospel.

Comment

This text probably derives from a period immediately after the Council of Nicaea, at which point Quartodecimans disappear from the catholic Church. The statement here prefaces a life of Polycarp, perhaps with the intention of repudiating any Quartodeciman claim in Smyrna on the basis of Polycarp's practice. The Phrygians, to whom reference is made here, are Montanists. This group was found mainly in rural Asia. They were Quartodeciman, in common with all other Asian Christians, but it appeared that because of their isolation they were unable to compute the time of Pascha, and so

[7] *The Life of Polycarp: An Anonymous Vita from Third-Century Smyrna,* A. Stewart-Sykes, ed. and trans., Early Christian Studies 4 (Sydney: St Paul's, 2002).

keep a solar Pascha, that is to say that they kept Pascha on a fixed date in a solar calendar, rather than the lunar calendar employed in Judaism. This would lead them to keep Pascha often outside the time of unleavened bread, namely the week following Pascha. Epiphanius (*Medicine Chest* 50.1) also records Quartodecimans in Asia who keep a solar Pascha. His account is very confused, but the confusions which had come about among the Quartodecimans at his time could be explained by the use of a solar calendar among isolated groups. It is significant that Epiphanius traces the origin of Quartodeciman practice to Montanism, an indication that the only Quartodecimans known in his day were Montanist.

E) A SELECTION RECONSTRUCTED FROM THE SYRIAN *DIDASCALIA* 21

Our Lord and teacher said when they asked him, "'Why are the disciples of John fasting, yet yours are not fasting?' In answer he said to them: 'The sons of the bridechamber cannot fast while the bridegroom is with them. But the days will come when the bridegroom will be taken from them, and in those days they shall fast'" (Mk 2.18–20). He is with us now by means of his operation, but is remote from our sight since he has ascended to the heights of heaven and is seated at the right hand of his Father. On this account you are to pray and intercede for them that are lost when you are fasting, as we also did when our Savior was suffering. So it is required of us to show pity to them, to have faith and to fast and to pray for them, as when our Lord came to the people, they did not believe in him when he taught them, but they let his teaching pass from their ears. Thus, since this people paid no heed, he accepted you brothers from the Gentiles and opened your ears for the obedience of the heart, just as our Lord and Savior himself said by means of Isaiah the prophet: "I appeared to those who asked not after me, and was found by those who sought me not, and I said 'I am here' to a people which called not upon my name" (Is 65.1). Now concerning whom did he speak thus? Was it not concerning the Gentiles, since they knew not God and were worshipping idols? When, however, our Lord came into the world teaching you, you that believed in him believed that God is one, and those who are worthy also shall believe until the number of those being saved shall be completed, "a thousand thousands and ten thousand times ten thousand" (Ps 67.18), as it is written in David.

However, he speaks thus of the people who did not believe in him: "I opened my hands all day long to a people that would not be persuaded and who resisted, who walk in a way which is not right, who go after their sins, which angers me in my sight" (Is 65.2–3). Thus observe that the people made the Lord angry by not believing in him, for which reason he says: "They made the Holy Spirit angry, and made themselves into enemies" (Is 63.10). And again, he speaks against them in another way through Isaiah the prophet: "Land of Zebulon, land of Napthali, the way of the sea, beyond Jordan, Galilee of the Gentiles, a people sitting in darkness, you have seen great light. And light has dawned on those who sit in darkness and in the shadow of death" (Is 9.1–2). He says "those who sit in darkness" concerning those of the people who came to believe in our Lord Jesus, for on account of the blindness of the people a great darkness was all around them, for they looked on Jesus but did not recognize him as the Messiah, and they understood him neither from the writings of the prophets nor from his works and his healings.However, we say to you of the people who have come to belief in Jesus that you may learn how the Scripture bears witness to us when it says, 'They have seen great light.' You who have believed in him have seen great light, Jesus Christ our Lord, as those who come to believe in him shall see.

However, those who sit in the shadows of death are you, you who are of the Gentiles, since you were in the shadows of death when you put your trust in the worship of idols and had no knowledge of God. Yet when Jesus Christ our Lord and teacher appeared, a light dawned upon you as you looked upon and put your trust in the promise of an everlasting Kingdom. You removed yourself far from the habitual conduct of former error, worshipping idols no longer, as you were worshipping, but long since have believed and been baptized in him, and a great light has dawned on you. Thus the people who paid no heed became darkness, but you who paid heed, you who are of the Gentiles, became the light. For this reason you are praying for them and interceding, most especially in the days of the Pascha, that they may find forgiveness through your prayers and return to the Lord Jesus Christ.

Thus it is required, brothers, that you investigate carefully in the days of the Pascha and perform your fasting with all diligence, making a beginning when your brothers from the people are keeping the Pascha. You shall observe it in this way whenever the fourteenth of the Pascha should occur, for neither the month nor the day falls at the same time each year, but is changeable. Thus you should be fasting when that people performs the Pascha; yet be careful to conclude your vigil within their [week of] unleavened bread.

Comment

The Syrian *Didascalia* gives instructions for the Pascha. In its present redaction it is not Quartodeciman, but there are clear signs that a document of Quartodeciman provenance has been included and worked over in the course of compiling the *Didascalia*, and the selection from the chapter published here follows my attempt to reconstruct that source.[8] Indications of Quartodeciman practice can be found in the anti-Judaism of the outlook of the vigil and in the concern that the Pascha be fixed in accordance with the Jewish Pesah. The chapter as presently redacted describes a pattern of vigil with prayer and fasting and with reading of Scripture, followed by joyful feasting and singing, which is exactly that to which Melito bears witness. *On Pascha* provides for a homiletic reflection on Scripture, followed by a celebration of Christ's resurrection triumph to accompany the feast. However, much of the Syrian *Didascalia* is

---

[8] *The Didascalia Apostolorum: An English Version with Introduction and Annotation* (Turnhout: Brepols, 2009).

the work of a further redactor; confusingly, this redactor, whilst not Quartodeciman, is heir to an originally Quartodeciman tradition! Thus there is still much in the chapter, beyond this source, which allows us to understand the atmosphere of the Quartodeciman vigil celebration.

f) From Theodoret's
Compendium of Heretical Tales 3.4 (PG 83.405)

The Quartodeciman heresy has this supposition: They say that the evangelist John preached in Asia and taught them to celebrate the feast of the Pascha on the fourteenth day of the moon. They have a defective understanding of the apostolic tradition, for they do not wait for the day of the Lord's resurrection but might keep the third day, or the fifth, or the Sabbath, or whatever day it might occur, and celebrate with praise the memory of the passion. Moreover, they employ falsified acts of apostles and other falsehoods far removed from grace, which they call "apocrypha."

Comment

Although roughly contemporary with Epiphanius, Theodoret is clearly far better informed. It is possible that Quartodeciman practice had lived on in his area of Syria. In particular, we should note the manner in which the Quartodecimans claim a Johannine tradition and a lunar Pascha, which is consonant with Melito's Christian tradition, the statement that the means of celebration is praise (actually he says "panegyric," which is a good description of *On Pascha* as rhetoric), the statement that the center of the feast is commemoration, and finally that the content of commemoration is actually the passion as much as the resurrection. The reference to falsified acts could well involve reference to the *Gospel of Peter*, with which Melito was certainly familiar and which seems to derive from a Quartodeciman milieu, since it presupposes a Johannine passion chronology and states that the apostles kept a fast whilst awaiting the resurrection.

G) *EPISTULA APOSTOLORUM* 15[9]

Ethiopic: "For you must keep the memorial of my death which is Passover; at that time they will throw one from among you who stand with me into prison for the sake of my name. And he will be exceedingly sad and distressed, for while you keep the Passover, he who will be in custody will not keep [it] with you. And I will send my power in the form of the angel Gabriel and the doors of the prison will open and he will emerge and come out to you that he might keep watch and rest together with you. After the cock crows [and] you have completed my agape and my memorial they will re-capture him and throw him into prison as a testimony until he shall go forth to preach just as I have commanded you." And we said to him, "O Lord, have you not completed the drink of Passover? Is it for us to accomplish a second time?" And he said to us, "Yes, until I come from the Father with my wounds."

Coptic: "And you commemorate my death. Now when the Passover takes place, then one from among you will be thrown into prison because of me. And he will be in grief and concern because you will keep the Passover while he is in prison and he is far away [from you]. For he will grieve because he did not keep the Passover with you. For I will send my power in the likeness of the angel Gabriel, and the doors of the prison will open. He will go out and come to you; he will spend a night of watch with you and stay with you until the cock crows. But when you complete my memorial and the agape, again he will be thrown into prison for a testimony, until he comes out and proclaims the things I have delivered to you." Then we said to him, "O Lord, is it again necessary that we take the cup and drink

[9]*Epistula Apostolorum* is extant in two different versions, one Ethiopic, the other Coptic. Both versions are given, translated by Fr Darrell Hannah, as part of his forthcoming commentary on the *Epistula*.

[from it]?" He said to us, "Yes, for it is necessary until a day when I come with those who were killed for my sake."

Comment

The points of interest in this text (which do not depend on conjectural reconstruction) are:

a) That the festival is kept in memory of the passion.

b) That a vigil forms part of the celebration.

c) That it is a night festival, complete by dawn.

d) That there is a commemorative meal-rite.

The significance of all of this in the reconstruction of the Quartodeciman celebration should be very clear.

The first part of the apostles' question, concerning the Lord's fulfillment of the Pascha, is not found in the Coptic version. However, it seems to reflect the same concerns about whether the feast is to be timed according to the Jewish celebration or after, that are reflected in the citations of Hippolytus and Apollinarius above.

Index of Ancient Authors
(apart from Melito)

Ps-Anarcharsis, 66*n*

Anastasius of Sinai, 20, 90

Apollinarius, 70*n*28, 101, 105–106, 108, 121

Aristotle, 24

Athenagoras, 18

Clement of Alexandria, 18, 21, 89

Clement of Rome, 13

Cornutus, 43–44

Didascalia (Syrian), 30, 35*n*, 38, 116–119

Dionysius of Halicarnassus, 60*n*14

Epiphanius, 116, 119

Epistula Apostolorum, 11, 35*n*40, 41, 120–121

Eusebius, 13–15, 17, 19–21, 39, 85–87, 88–89, 100, 101–102, 108–114

Heraclitus the grammarian, 44

Hesiod, 56*n*10

Hippolytus, 9, 32*n*29, 107–108, 121

Homer, 43, 56*n*10, 91–92

Irenaeus, 29, 96*n*6 and *n*8, 109, 111–114

Jerome, 102–103

Justin Martyr, 42, 67*n*, 87

Lucian, 16–17, 59*n*14

Maximus of Tyre, 44

Menander Rhetor, 87

Origen, 39, 89–90

Philo, 33–34, 75*n*36

Philostratus, 26*n*25, 42*n*

Pindar, 51*n*3

Plato, 59*n*14

Plutarch, 44

Polycarp (life of), 94, 115–116

Quintilian, 17–18, 44, 59*n*14

Tertullian, 39, 102–103

Theodoret, 119–120

Xenophon, 18–19

We hope this book has been enjoyable and edifying for your spiritual journey toward our Lord and Savior Jesus Christ.

One hundred percent of the net proceeds of all SVS Press sales directly support the mission of St Vladimir's Orthodox Theological Seminary to train priests, lay leaders, and scholars to be active apologists of the Orthodox Christian Faith. However, the proceeds only partially cover the operational costs of St Vladimir's Seminary. To meet our annual budget, we rely on the generosity of donors who are passionate about providing theological education and spiritual formation to the next generation of ordained and lay servant leaders in the Orthodox Church.

Donations are tax-deductible and can be made at www.svots.edu/donate. We greatly appreciate your generosity.

To engage more with St Vladimir's Orthodox Theological Seminary, please visit:

www.svots.edu
online.svots.edu
www.svspress.com
www.instituteofsacredarts.com

Index of Modern Authors

Ashton, J., 38*n*47

Bahr, G., 46

Barrett, C. K., 37

Bauckham, R., 15, 110*n*

Bauer, W., 18*n*

Bokser, B., 34

Bonner, C., 20–21, 39, 90

Cadman, W. H., 48

Carmichael, D. B., 46

Caulley, T. S., 100*n*19

Chrestos, P., 26*n*26

Daube, D., 69*n*27

Dorfmann-Lazarev, Igor, 35*n*39

Dugmore, C., 48

Gerlach, K., 56*n*11

Giulea, Dragoş-Andrei, 41*n*56, 45*n*

Gleason, M., 16, 18

Goehring, J., 20*n*20

Grant, R. M., 87*n*1, 91*n*

Guyot, P., 17

Hall, S. G., 9, 11, 14, 15, 22, 39*n*50, 40, 49, 50, 63*n*18, 70*n*28, 85, 87*n*22

Halton, T., 56*n*10

Hanfmann, G. M. A. and Buchwald, H., 47

Hanfmann, G. M. A., Yegül F., and Crawford J., , 47

Harvey, A. E., 72*n*31

Jeremias, J., 46

Jordan, H., 96*n*6

Kahle, P., 49

Kulp, J., 33*n*31, 34

Lawlor, H. E. and Oulton, W., 16

Leonhard, C., 36*n*41 and *n*43

Manis, A., 47

Mazza, E., 32

Mitten, D. G., 47

Nautin, P., 95

Nock, A. D., 92

Nodet E. and Taylor, J., 38

Perler, O., 49, 100

Pitra, J-B, 90, 92

Richard, M., 96*n*6, 99

Richardson, C. C., 48

Rosenblum, Jordan D., 34*n*36

Rouwhorst, G., 46

Rucker, I., 94, 96

Seager, A. R., 47

Stewart(-Sykes), A., 14*n*3, 22*n*22, 50*n*, 106*n*, 115*n*

Talley, T. J., 49

Testuz, M., 20*n*19

Too, Y. L., 19*n*14

Trebilco, P., 47

Trocmé, E., 46

Tsakonas, B. G., 47

Van Unnik, W. C., 75*n*35

Wahlde, U. C., 73*n*31

Wassermann, T., 100*n*18

Wellesz, E., 48

Werner, E., 38*n*46

Wifstrand, A., 47

Wilken, R., 94*n*

Wilson, S. G., 48

Zeitlin, S., 46

POPULAR PATRISTICS SERIES

1 *On the Priesthood* –
St John Chrysostom

2 *Lectures on the Christian Sacraments* –
St Cyril of Jerusalem

4 *On the Divine Images* –
St John of Damascus

6 *On the Holy Icons* –
St Theodore the Studite

7 *On Marriage and Family Life* –
St John Chrysostom

8 *On the Divine Liturgy* – St Germanus

9 *On Wealth and Poverty* –
St John Chrysostom

10 *Hymns on Paradise* –
St Ephrem the Syrian

11 *On Ascetical Life* – St Isaac of Nineveh

12 *On the Soul and Resurrection* –
St Gregory of Nyssa

13 *On the Unity of Christ* –
St Cyril of Alexandria

14 *On the Mystical Life*, vol. 1 –
St Symeon the New Theologian

15 *On the Mystical Life*, vol. 2 –
St Symeon the New Theologian

16 *On the Mystical Life*, vol. 3 –
St Symeon the New Theologian

17 *On the Apostolic Preaching* – St Irenaeus

18 *On the Dormition* –
Early Patristic Homilies

19 *On the Mother of God* – Jacob of Serug

21 *On God and Man* – Theological Poetry
of St Gregory of Nazianzus

23 *On God and Christ* –
St Gregory of Nazianzus

24 *Three Treatises on the Divine Images* –
St John of Damascus

25 *On the Cosmic Mystery of Christ* –
St Maximus the Confessor

26 *Letters from the Desert* –
Barsanuphius and John

27 *Four Desert Fathers* – Coptic Texts

28 *Saint Macarius the Spiritbearer* –
Coptic Texts

29 *On the Lord's Prayer* –
Tertullian, Cyprian, Origen

30 *On the Human Condition* –
St Basil the Great

31 *The Cult of the Saints* –
St John Chrysostom

32 *On the Church: Select Treatises* –
St Cyprian of Carthage

33 *On the Church: Select Letters* –
St Cyprian of Carthage

34 *The Book of Pastoral Rule* –
St Gregory the Great

35 *Wider Than Heaven* – Homilies
on the Mother of God

36 *Festal Orations* –
St Gregory of Nazianzus

37 *Counsels on the Spiritual Life* –
Mark the Monk

38 *On Social Justice* – St Basil the Great

39 *The Harp of Glory* – An African Akathist

40 *Divine Eros* –
St Symeon the New Theologian

41 *On the Two Ways* –
Foundational Texts in the Tradition

42 *On the Holy Spirit* – St Basil the Great

43 *Works on the Spirit* –
Athanasius and Didymus

44 *On the Incarnation* – St Athanasius

45 *Treasure-house of Mysteries* –
Poetry in the Syriac Tradition

46 *Poems on Scripture* –
St Gregory of Nazianzus

47 *On Christian Doctrine and Practice* –
St Basil the Great

48 *Light on the Mountain* – Homilies on the
Transfiguration

49 *The Letters* – St Ignatius of Antioch

50 *On Fasting and Feasts* – St Basil the Great

51 *On Christian Ethics* – St Basil the Great

52 *Give Me a Word* – The Desert Fathers

53 *Two Hundred Chapters on Theology* –
St Maximus the Confessor

54 *On the Apostolic Tradition* – Hippolytus

55 *On Pascha* – Melito of Sardis

ST VLADIMIR'S SEMINARY PRESS
1-800-204-2665 • www.svspress.com